Guitar Chord Songbook

Stevie Wonder

ISBN 978-1-4803-5075-5

HAL•LEONARD®
CORPORATION
7777 W. BLUEMOUND RD. P.O. BOX 13819 MILWAUKEE, WI 53213

Visit Hal Leonard Online at
www.halleonard.com

Guitar Chord Songbook

Contents

As

Words and Music
by Stevie Wonder

Do, do, do, __ do, do. Mm. _____

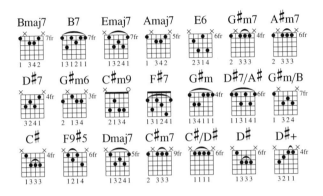

Intro

Bmaj7 B7   Emaj7
Do, do, do, do, do. Mm.

Bmaj7 B7   Emaj7
Do, do, do, do, do.

Verse 1

           Bmaj7   B7   Emaj7

As around ___ the sun the earth ___ knows she's revolv - ing,

        Bmaj7   Amaj7

And the rosebuds know to bloom in early May,

        Bmaj7   B7

Just as hate ___ knows love's the cure,

        Emaj7   E6

You can rest ___ your mind assure

        G#m7   A#m7 D#7 G#m7 G#m6 C#m9 F#7

That I'll ___ be loving you ___ al - ways.

Verse 2

Bmaj7   B7   Emaj7
As now   can't reveal the mys - t'ry of tomor - row,

Bmaj7   Amaj7
But in pass - ing will grow older ev'ry day,

Bmaj7   B7
Just as all ____ that's born is new,

Emaj7   E6
You know what ____ I say is true,

G#m7   A#m7   D#7
That I'll ____ be loving you ____ al - ways.

Chorus 1

G#m   D#7/A#   G#m/B   C#
(Until the rain - bow burns the stars ____ out in the sky.)

G#m   D#7/A#   G#m/B   C#
Always. ____ (Until the o - cean covers ev - 'ry mountain high.)

G#m   D#7/A#   G#m/B   C#
Always. ____ (Until the dol - phin flies and par - rots live at sea.)

G#m   D#7/A#   G#m/B   F9#5
Always. ____ (Until we dream ____ of life and life ____ becomes a dream.)

Verse 3

Emaj7   Bmaj7
Did you know that true love asks for noth - ing?

Emaj7   Dmaj7
Her acceptance is the way we pay.

Emaj7   Bmaj7
Did you know that life has given love ____ a guarantee

C#m7   C#/D#   D#   C#m9
To last through ____ forever and another day?

Verse 4

F#7   Bmaj7   B7   Emaj7
Just as time knew to move on ____ since the begin - ning,

Bmaj7   Amaj7
And the seasons know exactly when to change,

Bmaj7   B7
Just as kind - ness knows no shame,

Emaj7   E6
Know through all ____ your joy and pain

G#m7   A#m7   D#7   G#m7   G#m6   C#m9   F#7
That I'll ____ be loving you ____ al - ways.

Verse 5
Bmaj7   **B7**
As to - day I know I'm liv - ing,

    Emaj7   **Bmaj7**
But tomor - row could make me ___ the past,

           Amaj7
But that I mustn't fear;

    Bmaj7   **B7**
For I'll know ___ deep in my mind

    Emaj7   **E6**
The love of me ___ I've left behind,

  G♯m7   **A♯m7 D♯+**
'Cause I'll ___ be loving you ___ al - ways.

Chorus 2
  G♯m   **D♯7/A♯**   **G♯m/B**   **C♯**
(Until the day ___ is night and night ___ becomes the day.)

    G♯m   **D♯7/A♯**   **G♯m/B**   **C♯**
Always. ___ (Until the trees ___ and seas just up ___ and fly away.)

    G♯m   **D♯7/A♯**   **G♯m/B**   **C♯**
Always. __ (Until the day __ that eight times eight __ times eight is four.)

    G♯m   **D♯7/A♯**   **G♯m/B**   **C♯**
Always. ___ (Until the day ___ that is the day ___ that are no more.)

           G♯m
Did you know you're loved by somebody?

   D♯7/A♯   **G♯m/B**   **C♯**
(Until the day ___ the earth starts turn - ing right to left.)

    G♯m   **D♯7/A♯**   **G♯m/B**   **C♯**
Always. ___ (Until the earth ___ just for the sun ___ denies itself.)

    G♯m
I'll be loving you forever.

    D♯7/A♯   **G♯m/B**   **C♯**
(Until dear Moth - er Nature says ___ her work is through.)

    G♯m   **D♯7/A♯**   **G♯m/B**   **C♯**
Always. ___ (Until the day ___ that you are me ___ and I am you.)

    G♯m   **D♯7/A♯**   **G♯m/B**   **C♯**
Always. ___ (Until the rain - bow burns the stars ___ out in the sky.)

G♯m   **D♯7/A♯**   **G♯m/B**   **C♯**
(Until the o - cean covers ev - 'ry mountain high.) Always.

Instrumental   ‖: G#m   D#7/A# |G#m/B   C#   :‖ *Play 12 times*

Bridge

        G#m   D#7/A#   G#m/B
We all know some - times life's hates and trou - bles

C#   G#m
Can make you wish ___ you were born

    D#7/A#   G#m/B
In an - other time and space.

C#   G#m   D#7/A#   G#m/B
But you can bet ___ your life times that and twice it's dou - ble

C#   G#m   D#7/A#   G#m/B
That God knew ex - actly where He wanted you to be placed.

C#   G#m   D#7/A#   G#m/B
So make sure when you say you're in ___ it but not of ___ it

C#   G#m
You're not helping to make this earth

    D#7/A#   G#m/B
A place ___ sometimes called Hell.

C#   G#m   D#7/A#
Change your words ___ into truths ___ and then

      G#m/B   C#
Change that ___ truth into love,

        G#m
And maybe our children's grandchildren

   D#7/A#   G#m/B
And their great-great grandchildren will tell.

Chorus 3

        C#   G#m   D#7/A#
I've ___ been loving you ___ until the rain - bows

           G#m/B   C#
Burn the stars ___ out in the sky.

           G#m   D#7/A#   G#m/B   C#
‖: Loving you ___ until the o - cean covers ev'ry mountain high.

        G#m   D#7/A#   G#m/B   C#
Loving you ___ until the dol - phin flies and par - rots live at sea.

        G#m   D#7/A#
Loving you ___ until we dream ___ of life

     G#m/B   C#
And life ___ becomes a dream.

          G#m   D#7/A#
Been loving you ___ until the day ___ is night

      G#m/B   C#
And night ___ becomes the day.

         G#m   D#7/A#
Loving you ___ until the trees

         G#m/B   C#
And seas just up ___ and fly away.   :‖ *Repeat and fade*
                                                       w/ Vocal ad lib.

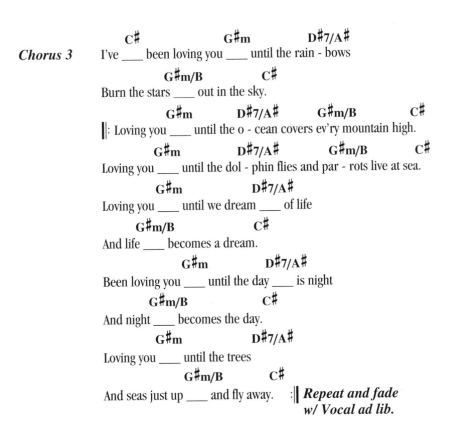

Boogie On Reggae Woman

Words and Music by
Stevie Wonder

Melody:

I like to see you boog-ie   right a-cross __

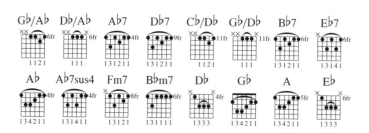

Gb/Ab Db/Ab Ab7 Db7 Cb/Db Gb/Db Bb7 Eb7

Ab Ab7sus4 Fm7 Bbm7 Db Gb A Eb

Intro

| N.C.   Gb/Ab Db/Ab |
||: Ab7   Gb/Ab Db/Ab :|| *Play 8 times*

Verse 1

Ab7   Gb/Ab   Db/Ab
I'd like to see you boog - ie

Ab7   Gb/Ab Db/Ab   Db7 Cb/Db Gb/Db Db7
Right across ___ the ___ floor.

Bb7
I like to do it to you

Eb7   Ab7 Gb/Ab Db/Ab Ab7   Gb/Ab Db/Ab
Till you holler for more.

Ab7   Gb/Ab Db/Ab
I like to reg - gae,

Ab7   Gb/Ab Db/Ab   Db7 Cb/Db Gb/Db Db7
But you dance too fast ___ for ___ me.

Bb7
I'd like to make love to you

Eb7   Ab7 Gb/Ab
So you can make me scream.

Chorus 1

A♭   A♭7sus4 Fm7 B♭m7
So, Boogie on,   Reggae Woman.

D♭   G♭
What is wrong with me?

 A♭ A   B♭7
Boogie on, Reggae Wom - an.

E♭   A♭7 G♭/A♭ D♭/A♭ A♭7 G♭/A♭ D♭/A♭
Baby, can you see?

Verse 2

A♭7   G♭/A♭ D♭/A♭
I'd like to see both of us

A♭7   G♭/A♭ D♭/A♭ D♭7 C♭/D♭ G♭/D♭ D♭7
Fall deeply ____ in ____ love.

B♭7
I'd like to see you and me

E♭7   A♭7
Under the stars above.

G♭/A♭ D♭/A♭ A♭7 G♭/A♭ D♭/A♭
Yes, I   would.

A♭7   G♭/A♭ D♭/A♭
I'd like to see both of ____ us

A♭7   G♭/A♭ D♭/A♭ D♭7 C♭/D♭ G♭/D♭ D♭7
Fall deeply ____ in ____ love.

B♭7
I'd like to see you in the raw

E♭7   A♭7 G♭/A♭
Under the stars above. Ah, ah.

Chorus 2

Ab   Ab7sus4 Fm7 Bbm7
So, Boogie on,   Reggae Woman.

Db   Gb
What is wrong with you?

     Ab A   Bb7
Boogie on, Reggae Wom - an.

Eb   Ab7 Gb/Ab Db/Ab Ab7 Gb/Ab Db/Ab
What you tryin' to do?

Harmonica Solo   *Repeat Verse 1 (Instrumental)*

Chorus 3

Ab   Ab7sus4 Fm7 Bbm7
Boogie on,   Reggae Woman.

Db   Gb
What is wrong with you?

     Ab A   Bb7
Boogie on, Reggae Wom - an.

Eb   Ab7 Gb/Ab Db/Ab
What you tryin' to do?

Ab   Ab7sus4 Fm7 Bbm7
Boogie on,   Reggae Woman.

Db   Gb
Let me do it to you.

     Ab A   Bb7
Boogie on, Reggae Wom - an.

Eb   Ab7
What you tryin' to do?

Outro
Harmonica Solo ‖: Ab7 Gb/Ab Db/Ab |Ab7   Gb/Ab Db/Ab |

                    |Db7 Cb/Db Gb/Db |Db7 |

                    |Bb7 |Eb7 |

                    |Ab7 Gb/Ab Db/Ab |Ab7   Gb/Ab Db/Ab :‖ *Repeat*
                                                                              and fade

Do I Do

Words and Music by
Stevie Wonder

Melody:

When _ I see _ ya on _ the street _

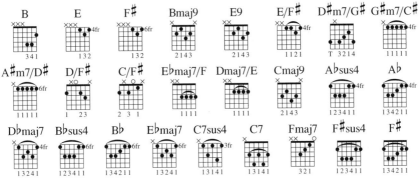

Intro   **B E F#** ‖: **Bmaj9** | | **E9** | **E/F#** :‖

                Bmaj9
Verse 1   When I see ____ ya on the street
                E9   **E/F#**
    My whole bod - y gets weak.
                Bmaj9
    When you're stand - ing in the crowd,
                E9   **E/F#**
    Your love talks ____ to me so loud.

                D#m7/G# G#m7/C# N.C. **A#m7/D# D#m7/G# G#m7/C#** N.C.
Chorus 1   Girl, do   I   do   what   you   do
    A#m7/D# D#m7/G# G#m7/C# N.C. **D#/F# C/F# Bmaj9 E9 E/F#**
    When   I   do,   my love _____ to you.

                Bmaj9
Verse 2   When I hear ____ ya on the phone
                E9   **E/F#**
    Your sweet sex - y voice turns my ear all the way on.
                Bmaj9
    Just a men - tion of your name
                E9   **E/F#**
    Seems to drive ____ my head insane.

Chorus 2

D#m7/G# G#m7/C# N.C. A#m7/D# D#m7/G# G#m7/C# N.C.
Girl, do   I   do   what   you   do

A#m7/D# D#m7/G# G#m7/C# N.C.   D#/F# C/F# Bmaj9
When   I   do,   my love _____ to you.

Ebmaj7/F Dmaj7/E E/F# Cmaj9
Baby.   Mm.

Bmaj9
Yes, ___ I got some candy kisses for your lips.

Ebmaj7/F
Yes, I got some honeysuckle, choc'late chips 'n' kisses

Dma7/E   E/F#   Cmaj9
Full of love for ___ you.

Bmaj9
Yes, ___ I got some candy kisses for your lips.

Ebmaj7/F
Yes, I got some honeysuckle, choc'late chips 'n' kisses

Dma7/E   E/F#
Full of love for ___ you.

Bridge 1

Absus4   Ab   Dbmaj7
My life has been waiting for your love.

Bbsus4   Bb   Ebmaj7
My arms have been waiting for your love ___ to arrive.

C7sus4   C7   Fmaj7
My heart has been waiting, my soul anticipating

F#sus4   F#
Your love, love, love.

Bass Solo 1 | N.C.(Bmaj9) | | E9 | E/F# |

Verse 3

Bmaj9
From the time ___ that I awake

E9   E/F#
I'm imagin - ing the good love that we'll make.

Bmaj9
If to me, ___ if I can do all this

E9
Well, just i - magine how it's gonna feel

E/F#
When we hug and ___ kiss, sugar.

Chorus 3   *Repeat Chorus 2*

Bridge 2   *Repeat Bridge 1*

Bass Solo 2 | N.C.(Bmaj9) | |(E9) |(E/F♯) |

Verse 4

       Bmaj9
I don't care ____ how long it might take,
       E9   E/F♯
'Cause I know ____ the woman for me, you I'll make.
       Bmaj9
And I will not deny myself the chance
       E9   E/F♯
Of being part ____ of what feels like the right ro - mance.

Chorus 4

       D♯m7/G♯ G♯m7/C♯ N.C. A♯m7/D♯ D♯m7/G♯ G♯m7/C♯ N.C.
Girl, do   I   do   what   you   do
A♯m7/D♯ D♯m7/G♯ G♯m7/C♯ N.C. D♯/F♯ C/F♯ Bmaj9
When   I   do,   my love _____ to you.
       E♭maj7/F Dmaj7/E E/F♯   Cmaj9
Oh yeah.   Oh.
       Bmaj9
||: Yes, ____ I got some candy kisses for your lips.
       E♭maj7/F
Yes, I got some honeysuckle, choc'late chip 'n' kisses
Dmaj7/E   E/F♯   Cmaj9
Full of love for ____ you.   :|| ***Repeat and fade***
                                   w/ vocal ad lib.

Castles in the Sand

Words and Music by Frank E. Wilson,
Hal Davis, Marcus Gordon, Jr. and
Mary Lazzara O'Brien

Melody:

Mm. _____ On the beach _____

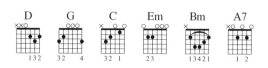

D   G   C   Em   Bm   A7

Intro

| D | | | | |

                                              Mm.

Verse 1

    G   C
On the beach

    D   Em   C
Where young ___ lovers meet,

    D   Em   C
You can see them there

            D   Em
As they sit and build

                G
Castles in the sand.

Verse 2

    G   C   D   Em
Heavenly, ___ she's so heavenly

    C   D   Em
    When she smiles at you

    C   D   Em
    And she helps you   build

                G
Castles in the sand.

Bridge

    C   G
The time comes when you stop pre - tending,

    C   G
For all dreams must come to an ending.

    Em   Bm
Re - member what happens to ___ castles of sand:

    A7   D
The sea will wash them a - way. Oh.

Verse 3

    G   C
And the beach

    D   Em   C
Where they ___ used to meet

    D   Em   C
  By the sand and sea

       D   Em
Waves have washed a - way.

Outro

            G   Em
Castles in the sand, castles in the sand.

         G7   Em
Where did they go? Castles in the sand.

                   G   Em
Tell me, where did they go?___ Castles in the sand.

                G
I wanna know where did they go? *Fade out*

Ebony and Ivory

Words and Music by
Paul McCartney

Melody:

Eb - o - ny __ and   i - vo - ry __

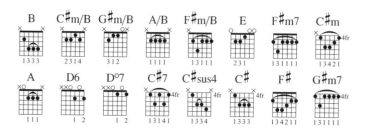

Intro

$\left|\right.$N.C.(B) C#m/B B G#m/B$\left|\right.$A/B F#m/B $\left|\right.$

Chorus 1

     E   F#m7
Ebony and ivory

     E   F#m7
Live to-gether in perfect harmony,

     E   F#m7
Side by side on my piano key - board,

B   E   N.C.(B) C#m/B B G#m/B A/B F#m/B
Oh, Lord, why ___ don't we?

Verse 1

E   C#m   B   A   E
     We all know that people are the same wher-ever you go.

                 B   D6   D°7
There is good and bad in ev - 'ryone, we learn to live

C#7   F#m7
And we learn to give each other what we need to survive,

A/B   E
To-gether alive.

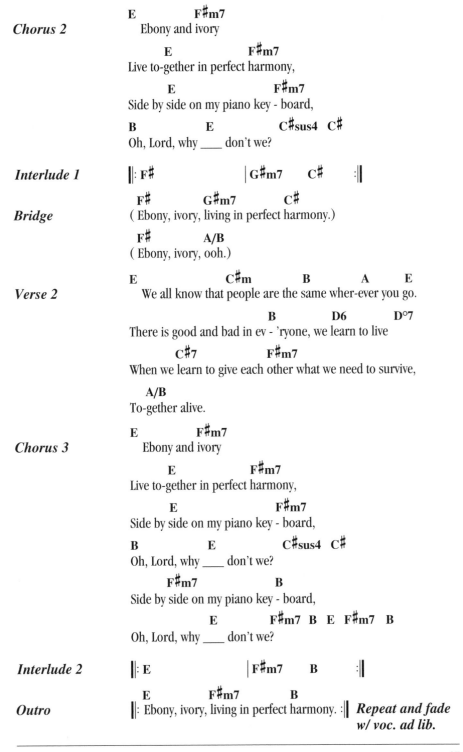

Chorus 2

   E   F#m7
   Ebony and ivory

     E   F#m7
   Live to-gether in perfect harmony,

     E   F#m7
   Side by side on my piano key - board,

   B   E   C#sus4 C#
   Oh, Lord, why ___ don't we?

Interlude 1 ‖: F# |G#m7 C# :‖

      F#   G#m7   C#
Bridge   (Ebony, ivory, living in perfect harmony.)

      F#   A/B
      (Ebony, ivory, ooh.)

      E   C#m   B   A   E
Verse 2   We all know that people are the same wher-ever you go.

           B   D6   D°7
   There is good and bad in ev - 'ryone, we learn to live

     C#7   F#m7
   When we learn to give each other what we need to survive,

    A/B
   To-gether alive.

Chorus 3

   E   F#m7
   Ebony and ivory

     E   F#m7
   Live to-gether in perfect harmony,

     E   F#m7
   Side by side on my piano key - board,

   B   E   C#sus4 C#
   Oh, Lord, why ___ don't we?

     F#m7   B
   Side by side on my piano key - board,

        E   F#m7 B E F#m7 B
   Oh, Lord, why ___ don't we?

Interlude 2 ‖: E |F#m7 B :‖

      E   F#m7   B
Outro ‖: Ebony, ivory, living in perfect harmony. :‖ *Repeat and fade*
                          w/ voc. ad lib.

For Once in My Life

Melody:

Words by Ronald Miller
Music by Orlando Murden

For once in __ my life   I have

Chord diagrams: F, F+, F6, D7♭9, Gm, D+, Gm7, Gm(maj7), C7, C+, B♭maj7, B♭6, Am, Dm, C7♭9, Fmaj7, Cm7, F9, G9, E♭, A♭, D♭, F♯, E, A, D, C♯7♭9, F♯+, F♯6, D♯7♭9, G♯m, D♯+, G♯m(maj7), G♯m7, C♯7, C♯+, Bmaj7, B6, A♯m, D♯m, C♯7♭9, C♯9, F♯maj7, C♯m7, G♯9, C♯7sus4

Intro   ‖: F | | :‖

Verse 1

     F   F+   F6   D7♭9
For once in my life I have someone who needs ___ me,

Gm   D+ Gm7 D+
Someone I need - ed so long.

   Gm   Gm(maj7) Gm7   C7
For once, unafraid, ___ I can go where life leads ___ me.

F   C+   F
Somehow I know ___ I'll be ___ strong.

            F+
For once I can touch what my heart used to dream of

B♭maj7   B♭6 F Am   Dm
Long before I knew, ___ oh, ___ someone warm like you

   Gm Am   B♭maj7
Would make my dream come true.

D7♭9   Gm7
Yeah, yeah, yeah.

Verse 2

C7♭9 Fmaj7   F+   F6   D7♭9
For   once my life   I won't let sorrow ___ hurt me,

Gm   C7
Not like it's hurt me before. ___ (Not like it's hurt before.)

           Gm   Gm(maj7)   Gm7   C7
For once ___ I have something I know ___ won't desert ___ me.

Fmaj7   F   Cm7
I'm not a - lone anymore.   (I'm not alone anymore.)

F9   F   F+
For once I can say this is mine, you can't take it.

  B♭maj7   G9
Long as I know I have love ___ I can make it.

   F   Dm   Gm   C7
For once in my life I have ___ someone who ___ needs me.

Interlude

N.C. (F)   (E♭)   (A♭) (D♭) (C7♭9)
(Someone ___ who needs me.

(F♯)   (E)   (A)   (D)   (C♯7♭9)
Someone ___ who needs me.)

Harmonica Solo |F# F#+ |F#6 D#7♭9 |G#m D#+ |G#m D#+ |

(For once in my

|G#m G#m(maj7) |G#m7 C#7 |F# C#+ |F# |

Life.)

| |F#+ | Bmaj7 | B6 |A#m |

|D#m |G#m A#m | Bmaj7   D#7♭9 G#m7

(Make my dreams come true.)

Verse 3

C#7♭9 F#   F#+   F#6   D#7♭9

For   once in my life, ___ I won't ___ let sorrow hurt me,

G#m   C#9

Not like it's hurt me before. ___ (Not like it's hurt before.)

G#m   G#m(maj7) G#m7   C#7

For once I have some - thing I know ___ won't desert ___ me.

F#maj7   F#6   C#m7

I'm not alone ___ any - more. (I'm not alone anymore.)

F#   F#+

For once I can say this is   mine, you can't take it.

Bmaj7   G#9

Long as I know I have love ___ I can make it.

F#   D#m   G#m7   C#7sus4

For once in my life, I have   someone who needs me.

Outro

N.C. (F#)   (E) (A)   (D) (C#7♭9)

‖: Someone who   needs me.   :‖ *Repeat and fade*

w/ lead vocal ad lib.

Heaven Help Us All

Words and Music by
Ronald Miller

Melody:

Heav-en help the child who nev-er had a home.

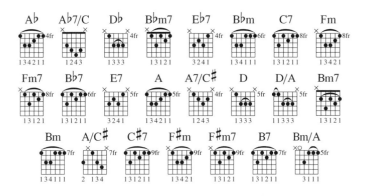

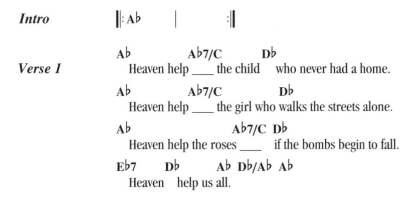

Intro   ‖: A♭ | :‖

Verse 1

A♭   A♭7/C   D♭
Heaven help ___ the child   who never had a home.

A♭   A♭7/C   D♭
Heaven help ___ the girl who walks the streets alone.

A♭   A♭7/C D♭
Heaven help the roses ___   if the bombs begin to fall.

E♭7   D♭   A♭ D♭/A♭ A♭
Heaven   help us all.

Verse 2

A♭   A♭7/C D♭
Heaven help the black ___ man if he struggles one more day.

A♭   A♭7/C   D♭
Heaven help the white ___ man if he turns ___ his back away.

A♭   A♭7/C D♭
Heaven help the man ___ who kicks the man who has to crawl.

E♭7 D♭ A♭
Heaven help us all.

Chorus 1

     B♭m7 A♭7/C D♭ E♭7
Heaven help us all.

A♭   B♭m7 A♭7/C D♭
Heaven help us all.

E♭7 A♭
Help us all.

   B♭m A♭ B♭m
Heaven help us, Lord.

C7   Fm Fm7 B♭7
Hear our call, when we fall.

   E♭7 N.C. E7
Oh, _____ yeah.

Verse 3

A   A7/C♯ D
Heaven help ___ the boy who won't reach twenty-one.

A   A7/C♯   D
Heaven help ___ the man who gave ___ that boy a gun.

A   A7/C♯   D
Heaven help the pe - ople with their backs against the wall.

E7   D   A
Lord, heaven ___ help us all.

    D/A A D/A A D/A
Heaven help us all.

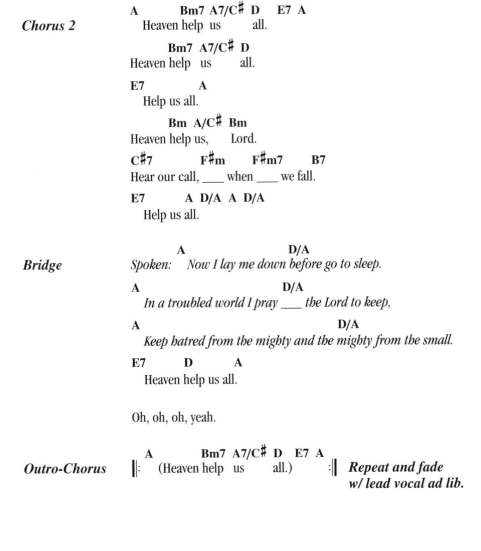

Chorus 2

A Bm7 A7/C# D E7 A
Heaven help us all.

   Bm7 A7/C# D
Heaven help us all.

E7   A
 Help us all.

   Bm A/C# Bm
Heaven help us, Lord.

C#7   F#m F#m7 B7
Hear our call, ___ when ___ we fall.

E7   A D/A A D/A
 Help us all.

Bridge

     A   D/A
Spoken: Now I lay me down before go to sleep.

A   D/A
 In a troubled world I pray ___ the Lord to keep,

A   D/A
 Keep hatred from the mighty and the mighty from the small.

E7   D A
 Heaven help us all.

Oh, oh, oh, yeah.

Outro-Chorus ‖: A   Bm7 A7/C# D E7 A   :‖ ***Repeat and fade***
         (Heaven help us all.)   ***w/ lead vocal ad lib.***

Higher Ground

Words and Music by
Stevie Wonder

Melody:

Peo-ple _   keep on   learn-in'.

Tune down 1/2 step:
(low to high) E♭-A♭-D♭-G♭-B♭-E♭

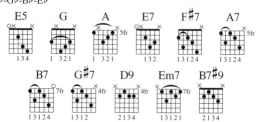

E5   G   A   E7   F♯7   A7

B7   G♯7   D9   Em7   B7♯9

| *Intro* | ‖: E5   G   A ｜E7   N.C. :‖ *Play 6 times* |

Verse 1

E5   G A
People

E7   N.C. E5   G A E7 N.C.
Keep on   learnin'.

E5   G A
Soldiers

E7   N.C. E5   G A
Keep on   warrin'.

E7 N.C.   F♯7 A7 B7
World

F♯7 G♯7   A7
Keep on turnin',

D9   E5 G A E7 N.C.
'Cause it won't be too long.

｜ E5   G   A ｜E7   N.C.   ｜

Verse 2

```
E5      G  A
Powers

E7    N.C. E5    G  A
  Keep on   lyin'

E7 N.C.         E5      G  A
  While your people

E7    N.C. E5    G  A
  Keep on   dyin'.

E7 N.C.    F#7 A7 B7
   World

F#7 G#7    A7
   Keep on turnin',

D9                    E5  G  A E7 N.C.
   'Cause it won't be too long.

| E5     G  A  | E7    N.C.        |
```

Chorus 1

```
        A7                Em7
I'm so darn glad he let me try it again,
        A7                Em7
'Cause my last time on earth I lived a whole world of sin.
        A7                Em7
I'm so glad that I know more than I knew then.
            F#7
Gonna keep ___ on tryin'
      B7#9                 E5   G  A E7 N.C. E5 G A E7 N.C.
Until ___ I reach my highest ground.
```

Verse 3

```
E5      G  A
Teachers.

E7    N.C. E5      G  A E7 N.C.
  Keep on   teachin'.

E5      G  A
Preachers,

E7    N.C. E5      G  A
  Keep on   preachin'.

E7 N.C.    F#7 A7 B7
   World,

F#7 G#7    A7
   Keep on turnin',

D9                    E5  G  A E7 N.C.
   'Cause it won't be too long.

| E5     G  A  | E7    N.C.        |
```

Verse 4

E5   G A
Lovers

E7   N.C. E5   G A
  Keep on   lovin'.

E7 N.C.   E5   G A
      Be - lievers

E7   N.C.   E5   G A E7 N.C.
  Keep on be - lievin'.

F$\sharp$7   A7 B7
Sleepers

F$\sharp$7 G$\sharp$7   A7
   Just stop sleepin',

D9   E5 G A E7 N.C.
  'Cause it won't be too long.

| E5   G   A |E7   N.C. |

Chorus 2

    A7   Em7
I'm so glad that he let me try it again,

      A7   Em7
'Cause my last time on earth I lived a whole world of sin.

    A7   Em7
I'm so glad that I know more than I knew then.

        F$\sharp$7
Gonna keep ____ on tryin'

  B7$\sharp$9   E5   G A E7 N.C.
Until ____ I reach my highest ground.

E5 G A   E7   N.C.   E5   G A E7 N.C.
      Till ____ I reach my highest ground.

| E5   G   A |E7   N.C. |

Outro   *Repeat Intro w/ lead vocal ad lib.*

I Just Called to Say I Love You

Words and Music by
Stevie Wonder

Melody:

No New   Year's Day

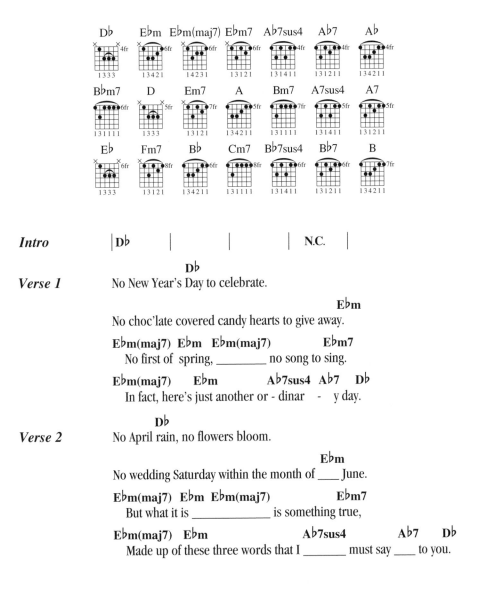

Intro | Db | | | N.C. |

<table>
<tr><td></td><td>Db</td></tr>
</table>

Verse 1   No New Year's Day to celebrate.

                                                   Ebm
No choc'late covered candy hearts to give away.

Ebm(maj7) Ebm Ebm(maj7)   Ebm7
No first of spring, _____ no song to sing.

Ebm(maj7)   Ebm   Ab7sus4 Ab7 Db
In fact, here's just another or - dinar - y day.

             Db
Verse 2   No April rain, no flowers bloom.

                                          Ebm
No wedding Saturday within the month of ____ June.

Ebm(maj7) Ebm Ebm(maj7)   Ebm7
But what it is _____ is something true,

Ebm(maj7)   Ebm   Ab7sus4   Ab7 Db
Made up of these three words that I _____ must say ___ to you.

Chorus 1

E♭m7   A♭   D♭
I just called ____ to say ____ I love ____ you.

E♭m7   A♭   B♭m7
I just called ____ to say ____ how much I care.

E♭m7   A♭   B♭m7
I just called ____ to say ____ I love ____ you.

E♭m7   A♭7sus4 A♭7 D♭
And I mean ____ it from the bot - tom of ____ my heart.

Verse 3

D♭
No summer's high, no warm July.

            E♭m
No harvest moon to light one tender August night.

E♭m(maj7) E♭m E♭m(maj7)   E♭m7
No autumn breeze, _____ no falling ____ leaves.

E♭m(maj7)   E♭m   A♭7sus4 A♭7   D♭
Not even time ____ for birds to fly ____ to ____ southern skies.

Verse 4

D♭
No Libra sun, no Halloween.

              E♭m
No giving thanks to all the Christmas joy you bring.

E♭m(maj7) E♭m E♭m(maj7)   E♭m7
But what it is, _____ though, oh, so new

E♭m(maj7)   E♭m   A♭7sus4   A♭7 D♭
To fill your heart ____ like no three words ____ could ev - er do.

Chorus 2

> D   Em7   A   D
> I just called ___ to say ___ I love ___ you.

> Em7   A   Bm7
> I just called ___ to say ___ how much I care. ___ I do.

> Em7   A   Bm7
> I just called ___ to say ___ I love ___ you.

> Em7   A7sus4   A7   D
> And I mean ___ it from the bot - tom of ___ my heart.

Chorus 3

> E♭   Fm7   B♭   E♭
> I just called ___ to say ___ I love ___ you.

> Fm7   B♭   Cm7
> I just called ___ to say ___ how much I care. ___ I do.

> Fm7   B♭   Cm7
> I just called ___ to say ___ I love ___ you.

> Fm7   B♭7sus4   B♭7   E♭
> And I mean ___ it from the bot - tom of ___ my heart,

> B   D♭   E♭
> Of my heart, baby, of my heart.

I Was Made to Love Her

Words and Music by Stevie Wonder,
Lula Mae Hardaway, Sylvia Moy and
Henry Cosby

Melody:

I was born _ in Lit - tle Rock

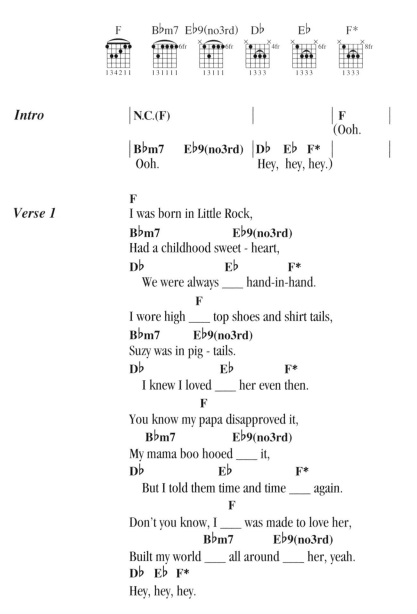

Intro | N.C.(F) | | F |
                                                    (Ooh.

| Bbm7   Eb9(no3rd) | Db Eb F* | |
  Ooh.   Hey, hey, hey.)

Verse 1

F
I was born in Little Rock,
Bbm7   Eb9(no3rd)
Had a childhood sweet - heart,
Db   Eb   F*
We were always ___ hand-in-hand.
            F
I wore high ___ top shoes and shirt tails,
Bbm7   Eb9(no3rd)
Suzy was in pig - tails.
Db   Eb   F*
I knew I loved ___ her even then.
            F
You know my papa disapproved it,
  Bbm7   Eb9(no3rd)
My mama boo hooed ___ it,
Db   Eb   F*
But I told them time and time ___ again.
            F
Don't you know, I ___ was made to love her,
              Bbm7   Eb9(no3rd)
Built my world ___ all around ___ her, yeah.
Db Eb F*
Hey, hey, hey.

Verse 2

                         F
She's been ___ my inspiration,

              B♭m7   **E♭9(no3rd)**
Showed ___ apprecia - tion

D♭   **E♭**   **F***
For the love I gave her through the years.

                        F
Like a sweet ___ magnolia tree,

              B♭m7   **E♭9(no3rd)**
My love blos - somed tender - ly.

D♭   **E♭**   **F***
My life grew sweeter through the years.

                      F
I know that my baby loves me,

   B♭m7   **E♭9(no3rd)**
My ___ baby needs me,

D♭   **E♭**   **F***
That's why we made it through the years.

           F
I was made to love her,

              B♭m7   **E♭9(no3rd)**
Worship ___ and adore ___ her.

D♭ E♭ F*
Hey, hey, hey.

                    F
Bridge   All through thick and thin, our love just won't end,

'Cause I love my baby, love, my baby. Hey!

Verse 3

F
My baby loves me,

Bbm7   **Eb9(no3rd)**
My baby needs ___ me,

   Db   **Eb**   **F***
And I ___ know I ain't going no - where.

     F
I was knee high to a chicken

         Bbm7   **Eb9(no3rd)**
When that love ___ bug bit me,

Db   **Eb**   **F***
   I had the fever with each pass - ing year.

       F
Oh, even if the mountain tumbles,

    Bbm7   **Eb9(no3rd)**
If this whole world crum - bles,

Db   **Eb**   **F***
   By her side I'll ___ still be stand - ing there.

       F
'Cause I was made to love her,

    Bbm7   **Eb9(no3rd)**
I was made to live for her.

Db **Eb** **F***
Hey, hey, hey. Ah!

Outro

     F
||:   I was made to love her,

         Bbm7   **Eb9(no3rd)**
Build my world ___ all around ___ her.

Db **Eb** **F***
  Hey, hey, hey.

       F
Ooh, baby, I was ___ made to please her.

     Bbm7   **Eb9(no3rd)**
You know Ste - vie ain't gonna leave ___ her, no.

Db **Eb** **F***
Hey, hey, hey. Oohey, baby.   :|| *Fade out*

I Wish

Words and Music by
Stevie Wonder

Melody:

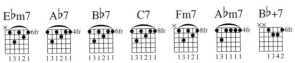

Look-ing back on when I ___ was a lit - tle nap - py head -

Ebm7   Ab7   Bb7   C7   Fm7   Abm7   Bb+7

Intro

| N.C.(Ebm7) (Ab7) | (Ebm7) (Ab7) | (Ebm7) (Ab7) | (Ebm7) Ebm7 Ab7 |
‖: Ebm7 Ab7 | Ebm7 Ab7 :‖

Verse 1

Ebm7
Looking back on

Ab7   Ebm7   Ab7   Ebm7 Ab7 Ebm7 Ab7
When I was a little nap - py headed boy.

Ebm7   Ab7
Then my only worry

Ebm7   Ab7   Ebm7 Ab7 Eb7 Ab7
Was for Christmas what ___ would be my toy.

Bb7   C7   Fm7   Abm7
Even though we sometime would not get a thing,

Bb7   C7   Fm7   Bb+7
We were happy with the joy that they would bring.

Ebm7   Ab7
Sneaking out the back door,

Ebm7   Ab7   Ebm7 Ab7 Ebm7 Ab7
To hang out with those hoodlum friends of mine,   ooh.

Ebm7   Ab7
Greeted at the back ___ door with,

Ebm7   Ab7   Ebm7 Ab7 Ebm7 Ab7
"Boy, I thought I told you not ___ to go outside."

Bb7   C7   Fm7   Abm7
Try'n' your best to bring the water to your eyes,

Bb7   C7   Fm7   Bb+7
Thinkin' it might stop her from whoppin' your behind.

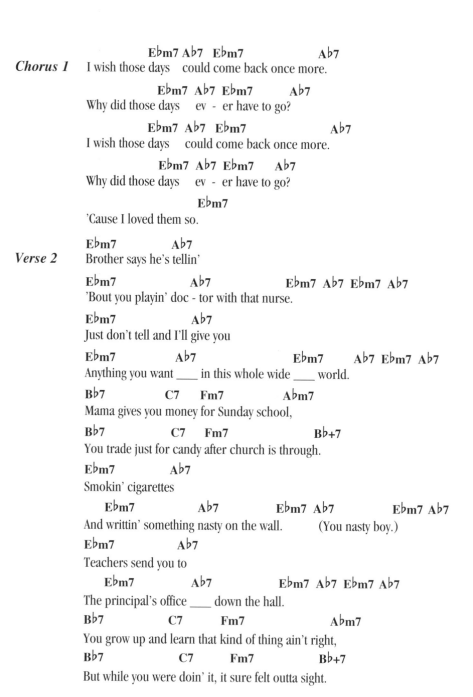

Ebm7 Ab7 Ebm7   Ab7

Chorus 1   I wish those days   could come back once more.

                 Ebm7 Ab7 Ebm7   Ab7

Why did those days   ev - er have to go?

              Ebm7 Ab7 Ebm7   Ab7

I wish those days   could come back once more.

              Ebm7 Ab7 Ebm7   Ab7

Why did those days   ev - er have to go?

                   Ebm7

'Cause I loved them so.

        Ebm7   Ab7

Verse 2   Brother says he's tellin'

Ebm7   Ab7   Ebm7 Ab7 Ebm7 Ab7

'Bout you playin' doc - tor with that nurse.

Ebm7   Ab7

Just don't tell and I'll give you

Ebm7   Ab7   Ebm7   Ab7 Ebm7 Ab7

Anything you want ___ in this whole wide ___ world.

Bb7   C7   Fm7   Abm7

Mama gives you money for Sunday school,

Bb7   C7   Fm7   Bb+7

You trade just for candy after church is through.

Ebm7   Ab7

Smokin' cigarettes

     Ebm7   Ab7   Ebm7 Ab7   Ebm7 Ab7

And writtin' something nasty on the wall.   (You nasty boy.)

Ebm7   Ab7

Teachers send you to

    Ebm7   Ab7   Ebm7 Ab7 Ebm7 Ab7

The principal's office ___ down the hall.

Bb7   C7   Fm7   Abm7

You grow up and learn that kind of thing ain't right,

Bb7   C7   Fm7   Bb+7

But while you were doin' it, it sure felt outta sight.

Chorus 2

E♭m7 A♭7 E♭m7   A♭7
I wish those days   could come back once more.

E♭m7 A♭7 E♭m7   A♭7
Why did those days   ev - er have to go?

E♭m7 A♭7 E♭m7   A♭7
I wish those days   could come back once more.

E♭m7 A♭7 E♭m7   A♭7
Why did those days   ev - er have to go? Ooh, hoo.

Interlude | E♭m7 A♭7 | E♭m7 A♭7 | E♭m7 A♭7 | E♭m7 A♭7 |

Outro   ‖: E♭m7 A♭7 | E♭m7 A♭7 :‖ *Play 16 times and fade*

I'm Wondering

Words and Music by
Stevie Wonder,
Sylvia Moy and
Henry Cosby

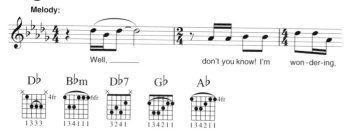

Intro
Db
Well, don't you know!

Chorus 1
Db   Bbm
I'm wondering, little girl, I'm wondering.

Db7   Gb
How can I make ___ you love me a little more than you loved him?

Db   Bbm
Oh, baby! I'm wondering, little girl, I'm wondering.

Db7   Gb
How can I make ___ you love me

A little more than you loved him? Oh, baby!

Verse 1
Db   Bbm
Jimmy was your sweetie pie, your pre - cious one,

Db7   Gb   Ab
And I knew ___ you used to love the very ground he walked upon.

Db   Bbm
One day Jim's papa told him things were look - ing down.

Db7   Gb   Ab
Then they packed ___ up ev'rything they owned and left ___ this little old town.

Db   Bbm   Db7
Each tear I cried for you, the clos - er our lives ___ grew.

Gb   Ab
I fell in love it's true, and you say ___ you love me too.

But baby…

Chorus 2   *Repeat Chorus 1*

         D♭   **B♭m**

Verse 2   The day you see his face again or hear ____ his voice,

D♭7   **G♭**   **A♭**

   I don't wanna be a loser if you have ____ to make a choice.

     D♭   **B♭m**   **D♭7**

   Like a puppet to a string, to you girl I'm at - tached,

            G♭   **A♭**

   And I know ____ I'd be in trouble if he came ____ and took you back.

     D♭   **B♭m**   **D♭7**

   I feel so insecure. In my mind ____ I can pic - ture

   G♭   **A♭**

   Los - ing you for sure, it's a pain ____ I can't endure.

                   D♭   **B♭m**

Chorus 3   And baby, I'm wondering, little girl, I'm wondering.

D♭7   **G♭**

   How can I make ____ you love me a little more than you loved him?

          D♭   **B♭m**

   Oh, baby! I'm wondering, sho' enough won - dering.

D♭7   **G♭**

   How can I make ____ you love me

   A little more than you loved him? Oh, baby!

Bridge
Db
I can't stop lovin' you, baby,

I can't stop lovin' you, girl.

I can't stop lovin' you, baby. Ooh.

Harmonica Solo ‖: Db | Bbm Db7 | Gb | Ab :‖

Verse 3
Db   Bbm   Db7
I feel so insecure. In my mind ___ I can picture
Gb   Ab
Los - ing you for sure, it's a pain ___ I can't endure.

Outro-Chorus
Db   Bbm
Baby, I'm worried. Really, really worried.
Db7   Gb
I wanna make ___ you happy, really, truly happy.
Db   Bbm
Baby, baby, I'm wondering, little girl, I'm wondering.
Db7   Gb
How can I make ___ you love me

A little more than you loved him? Oh, baby!
Db   Bbm
I'm wondering, little girl, I'm wondering. ***Fade out***

If You Really Love Me

Words and Music by
Stevie Wonder and Syreeta Wright

Melody:

If you real - ly love ___ me,

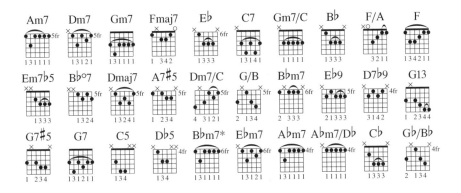

Intro

| Am7 Dm7 Gm7 | | Am7 Dm7 Gm7 | |
| Am7 Dm7 Gm7 | Fmaj7 | Eb | C7 | |

Chorus 1

    Am7 Dm7 Gm7
If you really love me,

        Am7   Dm7 Gm7
Won't you tell ___ me?

    Am7 Dm7 Gm7
And if you really love me,

        Am7   Dm7 Gm7
Won't you tell ___ me?

Gm7/C Bb   F/A   Gm7 F
Then, I won't have to   be

        Em7b5 Bb°7
Playing around.

Verse 1

       Dmaj7   **A7♯5**
You call my name, ooh, so sweet,

       Dmaj7   **A7♯5**
To make your kiss incomeplete.

   Dm7
When your mood is clear,

   Dm7/C   **G/B** **B♭m7 E♭9**
You quickly change your ways.

   Fmaj7
Then you say I'm untrue.

   Am7   **D7♭9**
What am I supposed to do,

  G13   **G7♯5** **G7**   **C5**
Be a fool who sits ____ a - lone waiting for you?

Chorus 2   *Repeat Chorus 1*

Verse 2

      Dmaj7   **A7♯5**
I see the light of your smile,

     Dmaj7 **A7♯5**
Calling me all the ____ while.

   Dm7   **Dm7/C**   **G/B B♭m7 E♭9**
You are saying, baby, ____ it's time to go.

   Fmaj7
First the feeling's all right,

   Am7   **D7♭9**
Then it's gone from sight,

  G13   **G7♯5**   **G7**   **C5**   **D♭5**
So I'm taking out this time ____ to say, ____ whoa,

Chorus 3
B♭m7* E♭m7 A♭m7
If you really love me,

        B♭m7* E♭m7 A♭m7
Won't you tell ___ me?

   B♭m7* E♭m7 A♭m7
And if you   really need me,

        B♭m7* E♭m7   A♭m7
Won't you tell ___   me? Baby, tell me

A♭m7/D♭ C♭   G♭/B♭ A♭m7 C♭
Then, I ___ won't have to be   playing around.

Outro-Chorus
B♭m7* E♭m7 A♭m7
‖: (If you   really love me,

        B♭m7*   E♭m7 A♭m7
Won't you tell ___ me?)   :‖ *Repeat and fade*
                                        w/ lead vocal ad lib.

Isn't She Lovely

Words and Music by
Stevie Wonder

Melody:

Is - n't she love - ly,

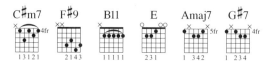

Intro

| N.C.(C♯m7) | (F♯9) | | (B11) | (E) | |

‖: C♯m7 | F♯9 | B11 | E :‖ *Play 3 times*

Verse 1

       C♯m7 F♯9   B11   E
Isn't she lovely,   isn't she wonderful?

       C♯m7 F♯9   B11   E
Isn't she precious,   less than one minute old?

        Amaj7   G♯7♯5
I never thought ___ through love we'd be

      C♯m7   F♯9
Making one as lovely as she.

       B11   E N.C.
But isn't she lovely, made from love?

Verse 2

$C\#m7$ $F\#9$ B11   E
Isn't she pretty,   truly the angels' best?

$C\#m7$ $F\#9$ B11   E
Boy, I'm so happy   we have been heaven blessed.

       Amaj7 $G\#7\#5$
I can't believe ___ what God has done;

     $C\#m7$ $F\#9$
Through us He's given life to one.

     B11   E N.C.
But isn't she lovely, made from love?

Harmonica Solo 1   *Repeat Verse 1 (Instrumental)*

Verse 3

$C\#m7$ $F\#9$ B11   E
Isn't she lovely,   life and love are the same.

$C\#m7$ $F\#9$ B11   E
Life is A - isha,   the meaning of her name.

      Amaj7 $G\#7\#5$
Londie, it could ___ not have been done

    $C\#m7$ $F\#9$
Without you who conceived the one.

     B11   E N.C.
That's so very lovely, made from love.

Harmonica Solo 2   *Repeat Verses till fade*

Keep On Running

Words and Music by
Stevie Wonder

Melody:

Some - thin' gon-na get cha.

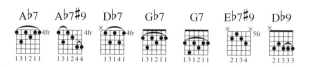

Ab7 Ab7#9 Db7 Gb7 G7 Eb7#9 Db9

Intro

N.C. Ab7
Somethin' gonna get cha. Somethin' gonna grab ya!

Somethin' gonna jump out of the bushes and grab ya!

A whole lotta folks, you better run faster. Somethin' gonna grab ya!

Somethin' gonna jump out of the bushes and grab ya!

Somethin' gonna grab ya! Oh, you need this thin' to grab ya, ha! Yeah, yeah.

Chorus 1

Ab7#9   Db7
You keep on runnin'. Keep on runnin' from my love.
Ab7#9   Db7
Keep on runnin'. Keep on runnin' from my love.

Verse 1

Ab7
Some folks say that you're really, really fine,
Db7   Gb7
All ___ you wanna be is just a friend of mine.
G7 Ab7#9   Eb7#9
But I know ___ the man you're with gonna break ___ your heart.
Ab7   N.C.
And you'll be sad real soon, yeah.

Chorus 2 *Repeat Chorus 1*

Verse 2

A♭7
Some folks say that you're really, really fine

D♭7   G♭7
But all ___ you want to be is just a friend of mine.

G7 A♭7♯9   E♭7♯9   A♭7 N.C.
But I know ___ I'm gonna get you in the end, real ___ soon.

Bridge

A♭7   D♭9
Why do you keep, (Keep on runnin', runnin' from my love?)

A♭7   D♭9
Keep on runnin' from (Keep on runnin', runnin' from my love.)

A♭7   D♭9
I need you, ba - by. (Keep on runnin', runnin' from my love.)

A♭7   D♭9
And ev'ry day, yeah. (Keep on runnin', runnin' from my love.)

Chorus 3 *Repeat Chorus 1*

Verse 3

A♭7
Some folks say that your love is really, really fine,

D♭7   G♭7
But all ___ you want to be is just a friend of mine.

G7 A♭7♯9   E♭7♯9
But I know ___ I'm gonna get ___ you in the end,

A♭7 N.C.
'Cause I need you so.

Outro

A♭7
‖: Keep on runnin'.

D♭9
(Keep on runnin', runnin' from my love.)

A♭7
Yeah, keep on runnin', ba - by.

D♭9
(Keep on runnin', runnin' from my love.) :‖ *Repeat and fade*
                w/ lead vocal ad lib.

Land of La La

Words and Music by
Stevie Wonder

You were brought up in a small town

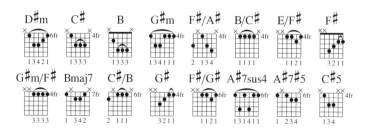

Chords: D#m C# B G#m F#/A# B/C# E/F# F#
13421 1333 1333 134111 2 134 1111 1121 3211

G#m/F# Bmaj7 C#/B G# F#/G# A#7sus4 A#7#5 C#5
3333 1 342 2 111 3211 1121 131411 1 234 134

Intro

‖: D#m | |C# | |

|B | |G#m F#/A# |B/C# :‖ *Play 4 times*

Verse 1

                 D#m
You were brought up in a small town
                 C#
Where ev'ryone is greeted   with a morning smile.
    B
I mean the place was so free from crime
             G#m   F#/A# B   B/C#
You could leave your   front door o - pen.
           D#m
And if your eyes were drawn from a lack of food
           C#
Or your pock - ets were short on cash,
           B
There was al - ways someone close at hand
         G#m F#/A#   B   B/C#
That you could   al - ways run ___ to.

E/F#   F#   G#m/F# F#
You could have been a   doctor

     E/F#   F#   G#m/F# F#
And you ___ could have been a nurse,

      Bmaj7   C#/B
But these things weren't

Bmaj7   C#/B   Bmaj7   C#/B Bmaj7 C#/B
Good e - nough for ___ you.

     G#   F#/G# G#   F#/G#   G#
So you   de - cided to pack up all ___ you own

      F#/G#   G# F#/G#
And get a one-way tick - et   there

G#   B/C#
To a place ___ where all the successful people went

A#7sus4   A#7#5
In order for them to do.

           D#m   C#
‖: I'm a big boy now, and she's a strong girl.

                             B
Remember only the strong can survive

             G#m F#/A# B/C#
Living in the land ____ of la _____ la. :‖

      D#m   C#
L.A.   L.A.   La, la, la, la.

         B
L.A. Hey, hey.

G#m F#/A# C#5
Land   of   la la.

    D#m   C#
L.A.   L.A.   La, la, la, la.

       B
L.A. Hey, hey.

     G#m F#/A# B/C#
The land   of   la la.

Verse 2

D#m
You get off ___ the bus,

C#
Pick up a paper and look ___ through the classified

B
So that you might find the place

G#m   F#/A#   B   B/C#
Suitable for   you to move in - to.

D#m
Then you turn around to pick up the duffle bag

C#
That you brought along,

B
But much ___ to your surprise,

G#m   F#/A#   B   B/C#
You find that bag has   taken off for walk - ing.

E/F#   F#   G#m/F# F#
 You dig in your wal - let

E/F#   F#   G#m/F# F#
To get   your last dime,

Bmaj7   C#/B   Bmaj7
But then re - call you just spent your last dime

C#/B   Bmaj7   C#/B Bmaj7 C#/B
On the news - paper.

G# F#/G#   G#   F#/G# G#
 You're much too pride - ful,

F#/G#   G# F#/G# G#
But pride has no de - fense

B/C#
When all ___ you've got in your possession

A#7sus4   A#7#5
Is the wallet in your hand.

Pre-Chorus 2

           D♯m   **C♯**
‖: I'm a big boy now, and she's a strong girl.

                                             B
Remember only the strong can survive

               G♯m F♯/A♯ B/C♯
Living in the land ____ of la _____ la. :‖ *Play 3 times*

Chorus 2

          D♯m   **C♯**
L.A.   L.A.   La, la, la, la.

          B
L.A. Hey, hey.

               G♯m F♯/A♯ B/C♯
Living in the land ____ of   la la.

Verse 3

              D♯m
You could get ev'rything you want,

        C♯
But not want ____ ev'rything you get

 B   **G♯m F♯/A♯ B/C♯**
Living in the land ____ of   la la.
D♯m   **C♯**
Being in la la land is like nowhere else.

 B   **G♯m F♯/A♯**
Living in the land, one hell of a land,

B/C♯
A land full of lost angels.

D♯m
Movie stars and great big cars and Perrier and fun all day

     C♯   **B**
And ____ that's enough to make anybody go ___ wild

        G♯m F♯/A♯ B/C♯
In the land of   la la.

Outro   *Repeat Pre-Chorus 1 and fade*

Living for the City

Words and Music by
Stevie Wonder

Melody:

A boy is born _ in hard time Mis - sis - sip - pi,

Tune down 1/2 step:
(low to high) E♭ - A♭ - D♭ - G♭ - B♭ - E♭

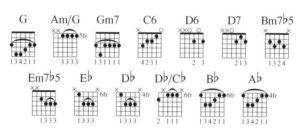

G   Am/G   Gm7   C6   D6   D7   Bm7♭5

Em7♭5   E♭   D♭   D♭/C♭   B♭   A♭

Intro

‖: G   Am/G Gm7 | Am/G   :‖

Verse 1

| G | Am/G Gm7 | | Am/G |
A boy is born   in hard time Missis - sippi,

G   Am/G Gm7   Am/G
Surrounded by   four walls that ain't so pret - ty.

G   Am/G Gm7   Am/G
His parents give   him love and affect - tion

G   Am/G Gm7
To keep him strong,   movin' in the right direction.

Chorus 1

           C6   D6   D7   G Am/G Gm7 Am/G
Livin' just enough, just e - nough for the cit - y.

Verse 2

G   Am/G Gm7   Am/G
His father works,   some days for fourteen hours,

G   Am/G Gm7   Am/G
And you can bet   he barely makes a dol - lar.

G   Am/G Gm7   Am/G
His mother goes,   scrub the floors for man - y,

G   Am/G Gm7   Am/G
And you best believe   she hardly gets a penny.

Chorus 2   *Repeat Chorus 1*

Interlude 1 | ¾ **Bm7♭5** | **Em7♭5** | **E♭** | **D♭** | **D♭/C♭** |
              | **B♭** | ²⁄₄ **A♭** | ⁴⁄₄ **G** | | |

Verse 3
G   Am/G   Gm7   Am/G
His sister's black,   but she is sho 'nuff pretty.

G   Am/G   Gm7   Am/G
Her skirt is short,   but Lord, her legs are stur - dy.

G   Am/G   Gm7   Am/G
To walk to school,   she's got to get up ear - ly.

G   Am/G   Gm7
Her clothes are old,   but never are they dirty.

Chorus 3   *Repeat Chorus 1*

Verse 4
G   Am/G   Gm7   Am/G
Her brother's smart,   he's got more sense than many.

G   Am/G   Gm7   Am/G
His patience long,   but soon he won't have an - y.

G   Am/G   Gm7   Am/G
To find a job   is like a haystack nee - dle,

G   Am/G   Gm7   Am/G
'Cause where he lives,   they don't use colored people.

Chorus 4
            C6
Livin' just enough,

D6   D7   G Am/G Gm7 Am/G G Am/G Gm7
Just e - nough for the cit - y.

Interlude 2 | ¾ **Bm7♭5** | **Em7♭5** | **E♭** | **D♭** | **D♭/C♭** |
              | **B♭** | ²⁄₄ **A♭** | ⁴⁄₄ **G** | | |
              | **G**   Am/G Gm7 | Am/G |

Outro
        G   Am/G Gm7   Am/G
‖: Livin' just e - nough for the city. Oh. :‖   *Repeat and fade w/ lead vocal ad lib.*

Master Blaster

Words and Music by
Stevie Wonder

Melody:

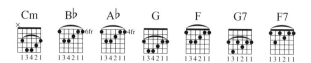

Ev - 'ry - one's feel-ing pret-ty,

| Cm | B♭ | A♭ | G | F | G7 | F7 |

Intro

N.C.(Cm)	(B♭)	(A♭)	(G)
(F)		(Cm)	(B♭)
: (Cm)	B♭	A♭	G
F		Cm	B♭ :

Verse 1

    Cm   B♭
Ev'ryone's feeling pretty,

A♭   G
It's hotter than July.

F
Though the world's full of problems

        Cm   B♭
They couldn't touch us even if they tried.

Cm   B♭
From the park I hear rhythms;

A♭   G
Marley's hot on the box.

F
Tonight there will be a party,

      Cm   B♭
On the corner at the end of the block.

Chorus 1

       Cm   **G7**   **F7**
Didn't know you would be jammin' until the break of dawn.

N.C.(Cm)   **Cm**
I'll bet you nobody ever told you that you

G7   **F7**
Would be jammin' until the break of dawn.

N.C.(Cm)
You would be jammin' and jammin' and jammin' and jam on.

Ah, ha, oh.

Verse 2

Cm   **B♭**
   They want us to join the fighting,

A♭   **G**
   But our answer today

F
   Is to let all our worries,

   Cm   **B♭**
Like the breeze through our fingers, slip away.

Cm   **B♭**
   Peace has come to Zimbabwe,

A♭   **G**
   Third world's right on the one.

F
   Now's the time for celebration,

   Cm   **B♭**
'Cause we've only just begun.

Chorus 2

       Cm   **G7**   **F7**
Didn't know you would be jammin' until the break of dawn.

   N.C.(Cm)   **Cm**
‖: I'll bet you nobody ever told you that you

G7   **F7**
Would be jammin' until the break of dawn. :‖

N.C.(Cm)   **Cm**
I know nobody told you that you

G7   **F7**
Would be jammin' until the break of dawn,

   N.C.(Cm)
But we're jammin', jammin', jammin', jam on.

Interlude

|N.C.(Cm) | | | |

| | | | |

                Heh, heh.   Woo!
| | (B♭) |(A♭) | (G) |

   Woo!
|(F) | |(Cm) |(B♭) |

Verse 3

Cm   B♭
You ask me, am I happy.
A♭   G
Well, as a matter of fact,
F
I can say that I'm ecstatic
     Cm   B♭
'Cause we all just made a pact.
Cm   B♭
We've agreed to get together,
A♭   G
Join as children in Jah.
F
When you're moving in the positive,
     Cm   B♭
Your destina - tion is the brightest star.

Chorus 3

                    Cm   G7   F7
You didn't know that you would be jammin' until the break of dawn.
   N.C.(Cm)   Cm
I'll bet you nobody ever told you that you
   G7   F7
Would be jammin' until the break of dawn.
N.C.(Cm)
Oh, woh, woh.
Cm   G7   F7
You would be jammin' until the break of dawn.
N.C.(Cm)
Don't you stop the music, oh.

Outro-Chorus

   Cm   G7
‖: (We're in the middle of the makin's
                F7   N.C.(Cm)
Of the master blaster jammin'.)   :‖ *Repeat and fade*
                                          w/ lead vocal ad lib.

My Love

Words and Music by
Stevie Wonder

Melody:

My __ love is ___   warm-er than _ a smile. __

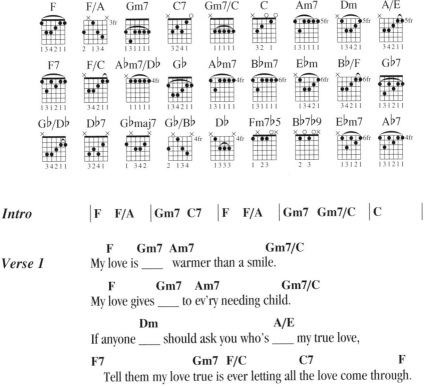

Intro

| F F/A | Gm7 C7 | F F/A | Gm7 Gm7/C | C | |

Verse 1

    F   Gm7 Am7   Gm7/C
My love is ___ warmer than a smile.

    F   Gm7 Am7   Gm7/C
My love gives ___ to ev'ry needing child.

            Dm   A/E
If anyone ___ should ask you who's ___ my true love,

F7   Gm7 F/C   C7   F
   Tell them my love true is ever letting all the love come through.

Verse 2

A♭m7/D♭ G♭   A♭m7 B♭m7   A♭m7/D♭
   My love sees ___ love with not a face,

G♭   A♭m7 B♭m7   A♭m7/D♭
And lives to ___ love through time and space.

E♭m   B♭/F   G♭7   A♭m7
If all of ev'rything about ___ my love fits to the tune of you,

G♭/D♭   D♭7   G♭
Then you can say that you are ___ my love, too.

Chorus 1

Gb   Gbmaj7
Let my love shine throughout the world

Abm7   Gb   Gb/Bb   Db
To ev'ry moun - tain top   and stee - ple.

Fm7b5   Bb7b9   Ebm7   Ab7   Abm7/Db
Let it be felt ___ by ev'ry soul ___ 'till love's all o - ver.

Gb   Gbmaj7
Let it reach out to ev'ry heart,

Abm7   Gb   Gb/Bb   Db
To ev'ry dis - enfran - chised peo - ple,

Fm7b5   Bb7b9   Ebm7   Ab7   Abm7/Db   Gb
Till it is pres - ent and no more ___ is pain all o - ver.

Verse 3

Gb   Abm7   Bbm7   Abm7/Db
Our love sees ___ love's the key to peace,

Gb   Abm7   Bbm7   Abm7/Db
We'll pray till ___ all ___ world wars have ceased.

Ebm   Bb/F
Should you or an - yone you know ___ enough

Gb7   Abm7
To say ___ they feel as we,

Gb/Db   Db7   Gb
Then let our univer - sal song be free.

Chorus 2

Gb   Gbmaj7
Let our love shine throughout the world

Abm7   Gb   Gb/Bb   Db
To ev'ry moun - tain top   and stee - ple.

Fm7b5   Bb7b9   Ebm7   Ab7   Abm7/Db   Gb   Db
Let it be felt ___ by ev'ry soul ___ till love's all o - ver.

Harmonica Solo |Gb   Gbmaj7 |Abm7 Gb Gb/Bb |Db |
|Fm7b5 Bb7b9 |Ebm7 |Ab7 |
|Abm7/Db |

Chorus 3

Gb   Gbmaj7
Say words of love to all we see.

Abm7   Gb   Gb/Bb   Db
To rich or poor, ___ for love ___ is e - qual.

Fm7b5   Bb7b9   Ebm7   Ab7   Abm7/Db
Let us lift up ___ humanity, ___ spread love all o - ver.

Gb   Gbmaj7
Let all its forces join as one,

Abm7   Gb   Gb/Bb   Db
So to rebuke ___ all signs of e - vil,

Fm7b5   Bb7b9   Ebm7
Through ev'ry val - ley, land and sea

Ab7   Abm7/Db Gb   Db
Our love's all peo - ple.

Outro-
Harmonica Solo   ‖: Gb   Gbmaj7 |Abm7 Gb Gb/Bb |
|Db |Fm7b5 Bb7b9 |
|Ebm7 |Ab7 |
|²⁄₄ Abm7/Db |⁴⁄₄ Gb   Db   :‖ *Repeat and fade*

My Cherie Amour

Words and Music by Stevie Wonder,
Sylvia Moy and Henry Cosby

Melody:

La, la,   la,   la, __   la,   la.

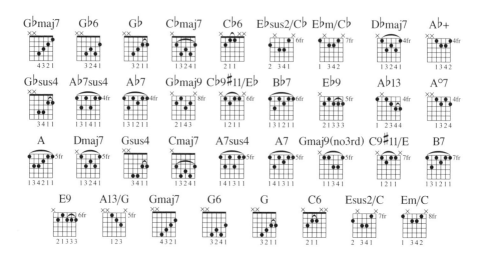

Intro   N.C.| G♭maj7 G♭6 G♭ | C♭maj7 C♭6 C♭maj7 | E♭sus2/C♭ E♭m/C♭ |
    | D♭maj7 N.C. G♭maj7 G♭6 G♭ C♭maj7
    La, la, la,   la,   la,   la.

    C♭6 C♭maj7 E♭sus2/C♭ E♭m/C♭ D♭ma7
    La,   la,   la,   la, la,   la.

    A♭+   D♭maj7   G♭sus4   C♭maj7 A♭7sus4 A♭7
Chorus 1   My Che - rie Amour, lovely as a summer day.

    D♭maj7   G♭sus4   C♭maj7 A♭7sus4 A♭7
    My Che - rie Amour, distant as the Milky Way.

    G♭maj9   A♭7sus4 A♭7   C♭9♯11/E♭
    My Che - rie Amour, pretty little one that I ___ adore,

    B♭7   E♭9
    You're the only girl my heart ___ beats for.

    A♭13   A♭7   D♭maj7
    How I wish that you ___ were mine.

Verse 1

A°7   D♭maj7 G♭sus4   C♭maj7 A♭7sus4
In a   café or   sometimes on a crowded street,

A♭7   D♭maj7   G♭sus4   C♭maj7 A♭7sus4 A♭7
I've been near you but you never noticed me.

Gbmaj9   A♭7sus4   A♭7   C♭9#11/E♭
My Che - rie Amour, won't you tell me how could you ____ ignore,

B♭7   E♭9
That behind that little smile ____ I wore,

A♭13   A♭7   D♭maj7
How I wish that you were ____ mine.

Interlude

        N.C. G♭maj7 G♭6 G♭ C♭maj7
‖: La, la, la,   la,   la, la.

C♭6 C♭maj7 E♭sus2/C♭ E♭m/C♭ D♭ma7
La,   la,   la,   la, la,   la.   :‖

Verse 2

        A   Dmaj7   Gsus4   Cmaj7
Maybe someday, you'll see my face among the crowd.

A7sus4 A7   Dmaj7   Gsus4   Cmaj7 A7sus4
May -   be someday, I'll share your little distant cloud.

        A7   Gmaj9(no3rd) A7sus4   A7   C9#11/E
Oh, ____ Che - rie Amour,   pretty little one that I ____ adore

        B7   E9
You're ____ the only girl my heart ____ beats for.

A13/G   A7   Dmaj7
How I wish that you were mine.

Outro

        N.C. Gmaj7 G6 G Cmaj7
‖: La, la, la,   la,   la, la.

C6 Cmaj7 Esus2/C Em/C Dmaj7
La,   la,   la,   la, la, la.   :‖   *Repeat and fade*

Never Had a Dream Come True

Words and Music by Stevie Wonder,
Sylvia Moy and Henry Cosby

Melody:

Do, do,   do, do,   do, do, ___ do,

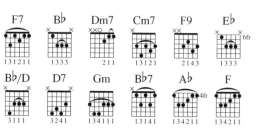

Intro

N.C. **F7 B♭**
Do, do, do, do,

Dm7   Cm7
Do, do, do, do, do,

F9   B♭
Do, do, do.

F7 B♭
Do, do, do, do,

Dm7   Cm7
Do, do, do, do, do,

F9   B♭
Do, do, do.

Verse 1

E♭   **B♭/D D7**   **Gm B♭7**
I never, never had a dream come true.

E♭   **B♭/D D7**   **Gm B♭7**
In my ev'ry dream   I'm loved by you,

A♭   **E♭**
And we're free as ___ the wind,

A♭   **E♭**
And true love is no sin.

A♭   **E♭**   **F**   **B♭7**
Therefore, men are men, not machines.

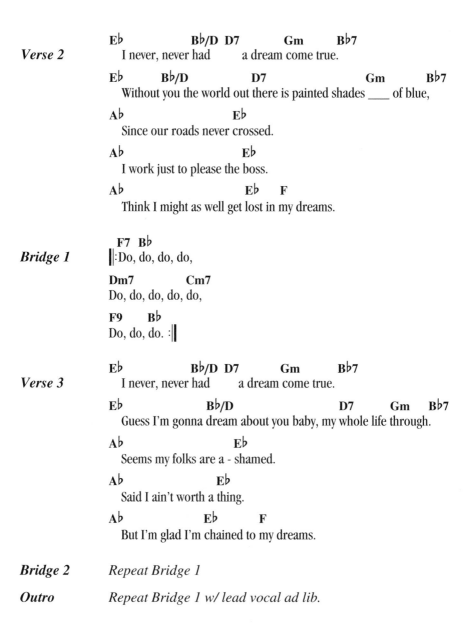

Verse 2

E♭   B♭/D   D7   Gm   B♭7
I never, never had   a dream come true.

E♭   B♭/D   D7   Gm   B♭7
Without you the world out there is painted shades ___ of blue,

A♭   E♭
Since our roads never crossed.

A♭   E♭
I work just to please the boss.

A♭   E♭   F
Think I might as well get lost in my dreams.

Bridge 1

F7   B♭
‖:Do, do, do, do,

Dm7   Cm7
Do, do, do, do, do,

F9   B♭
Do, do, do. :‖

Verse 3

E♭   B♭/D   D7   Gm   B♭7
I never, never had   a dream come true.

E♭   B♭/D   D7   Gm   B♭7
Guess I'm gonna dream about you baby, my whole life through.

A♭   E♭
Seems my folks are a - shamed.

A♭   E♭
Said I ain't worth a thing.

A♭   E♭   F
But I'm glad I'm chained to my dreams.

Bridge 2   *Repeat Bridge 1*

Outro   *Repeat Bridge 1 w/ lead vocal ad lib.*

Nothing's Too Good for My Baby

Words and Music by Sylvia Moy,
Henry Cosby and William Stevenson

Melody:

Noth-in's too good _ for my ba - by. __

Bb   Ab/Bb   Cm   Db   F

Intro | N.C.(Bb) | | | |

                                                              Hey!

Chorus 1

       Bb   **Ab/Bb**

‖: Nothin's too good for my baby.

       Bb   **Ab/Bb**

Nothin's too good for my girl. :‖

Verse 1

         Bb   **Ab/Bb**

I'm ___ the luckiest guy in the world,

        Bb   **Ab/Bb**

'Cause I've got one pearl of a girl.

        Bb   **Ab/Bb**

For ___ my baby I work part time

         Bb   **Ab/Bb**

Down ___ at the neighborhood five and dime.

        Bb   **Ab/Bb**

Half ___ of my money goes to buy her

         Bb   **Ab/Bb**

Some ___ of the things her little heart desires.

       Bb   **Ab/Bb**

The other half goes dime by dime,

       Bb   **Ab/Bb**

To show my cookie a real good time.

Chorus 2   *Repeat Chorus 1*

Bridge 1

     Cm
She's ___ sweet and she's fine,

     B♭
And she tells ___ me that she's mine, all mine.

  D♭
Now ain't that loving, ain't that living,

  F
Ain't that worth a world of giving?

Chorus 3   *Repeat Chorus 1*

     B♭   **A♭/B♭**
Verse 2   I ___ walk around with my chest stuck out

    B♭   **A♭/B♭**
'Cause my baby's worth bragging about.

     B♭   **A♭/B♭**
Ev - 'ry Johnny, Jack, and Jim

      B♭   **A♭/B♭**
Wished ___ that she belonged to him.

    B♭   **A♭/B♭**
I ___ gave up the old gang of mine

       B♭   **A♭/B♭**
'Cause with ___ my girl goes all my time.

  B♭   **A♭/B♭**
One of these days I'm gonna buy a ring

     B♭   **A♭/B♭**
And marry her and ev'rything.

Chorus 4   *Repeat Chorus 1*

      Cm
Bridge 2   She's ___ sweet and she's mellow

       B♭
And she tells ___ me that I am one heck of a fellow.

   D♭
Now ain't that loving, ain't that living,

  F
Ain't that worth a world of giving?

Outro-Chorus *Repeat Chorus 1 and fade*

Overjoyed

Words and Music by
Stevie Wonder

Melody:

O - ver time __

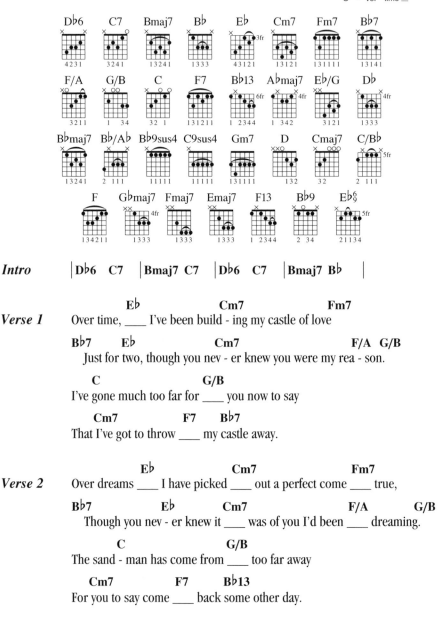

Intro | Db6 C7 | Bmaj7 C7 | Db6 C7 | Bmaj7 Bb |

Verse 1

            Eb   Cm7   Fm7
Over time, ___ I've been build - ing my castle of love

Bb7   Eb   Cm7   F/A G/B
Just for two, though you nev - er knew you were my rea - son.

       C   G/B
I've gone much too far for ___ you now to say

    Cm7   F7   Bb7
That I've got to throw ___ my castle away.

Verse 2

            Eb   Cm7   Fm7
Over dreams ___ I have picked ___ out a perfect come ___ true,

Bb7   Eb   Cm7   F/A   G/B
Though you nev - er knew it ___ was of you I'd been ___ dreaming.

         C   G/B
The sand - man has come from ___ too far away

    Cm7   F7   Bb13
For you to say come ___ back some other day.

Chorus 1

                                    Abmaj7   Eb/G
And though you don't be - lieve that they do, they do come true,

Fm7   Bb7   Db   C
For did my dreams ___ come true when I looked at you.

               Bbmaj7   F/A   Bb/Ab   Fm7
It may be true if you would believe, you, too, might be ___ overjoyed,

               Bb9sus4 Bb7 Db6   C7 Bmaj7 C7 Db6 C7 Bmaj7 Bb
Over loved, ___ o - ver ___ me.

Verse 3

                     Eb   Cm7   Fm7
Over hearts ___ I have pain - fully turned ev'ry ___ stone

Bb7   Eb   Cm7   F/A G/B
  Just to ___ find I have found ___ what I've searched to discov - er.

          C   G/B
I've come ___ much too far for ___ me now to find

    Cm7   F7   Bb13
The love that I sought ___ can never be mine.

Chorus 2

                                   Abmaj7   Eb/G
And though you don't be - lieve that they do, they do come true,

Fm7   Bb7   Db   C
For did my dreams ___ come true when I looked at you.

               Bbmaj7   F/A   Bb/Ab   Fm7
It may be true if you would believe, you, too, might be ___ overjoyed,

               Bb9sus4 Bb7   C9sus4
Over love ___   over me.

Chorus 3

        C7   Bbmaj7   F/A
  And though they might say "improbable," what ___ do they know?

Gm7   C7   Eb   D
For in romance, ___ all true love needs is a chance,

                Cmaj7
And maybe with a chance you will find

     G/B   C/Bb   Gm7
You, ___ too, like I'm ___ overjoyed,

           C9sus4 C7   F Gbmaj7 Fmaj7 Emaj7
Over loved, ___ o - ver you,

F13 Bb9 Eb§
O - ver you.

Part Time Lover

Words and Music by
Stevie Wonder

Melody:

Call up, ring once, hang up ___ the phone ___

(Capo 1st fret)

Am7   G   Fmaj7   Em7   Dm7   Gm7   C   F   F#m7b5   E7sus4

Intro

| Am7 | G | Fmaj7 | Em7 |
| Dm7 | Em7 | Am7 | Dm7 Em7 |

Am7   G
Ooh, ____ do, do, da, da, da, da, da, da.

Fmaj7   Em7
Do, da, da, da, da, da, da, da, da.

Dm7   Em7   Am7
Do, do, do, da, ____da, da, da, da, da, da, da.

Verse 1

Dm7 Em7 Am7
Call up, ring once, hang up the phone

G Fmaj7
To let me know you made it home.

Em7   Dm7   Em7 Am7
Don't want nothin' to be wrong with part time lover.

If she's with me, I'll blink the lights

G Fmaj7
To let you know tonight's the night

Em7 Dm7 Em7 Am7
For me and you, my part time lover.

Chorus 1

Gm7 C F   C
We   are undercover passion on the run,

       Dm7   Em7 F#m7♭5 G Am7
Chasing love up against the sun.

Gm7 C F   C
We   are strangers by day, lovers by night,

          Dm7   E7sus4
Knowing it's so wrong, but feeling so right.

Verse 2

          Am7
If I'm with friends and we should meet,

     G   Fmaj7
Just pass me by, ___ don't even speak.

      Em7   Dm7   Em7   Am7
Know the word dis - creet when part time lovers.

But if there's some emergency,

     G   Fmaj7
Have a male friend to ask for me

      Em7   Dm7   Em7   Am7
So then ___ she won't be to you my part time lover.

Chorus 2   *Repeat Chorus 1*

Interlude

Am7   G
  Da, da, da, da, da, da, da, da.

Fmaj7   Em7
  Da, da, da, da, da, da, da, da, da.

Dm7   Em7   Am7   Dm7 Em7
  Do, do, do, dum, ___ dum, da, da, da, da, da, da, da.

Am7   G
  Da, da, da, da, da, da, da, da.

Fmaj7   Em7
  Da, da, da, da, da, da, da, da, da.

Dm7   Em7   Am7
  Do, do, do, dum, ___ dum, da, da, da, da, da, da, da.

Chorus 3   *Repeat Chorus 1*

Verse 3

                        Am7
                 I've got some - thing that I must tell,

                        G   **Fmaj7**
                 Last night ____ some - one rang our doorbell

                     Em7   **Dm7**   **Em7**   **Am7**
                 And it was not you, my part time lover.

                 And then a man called our exchange,

                     G   **Fmaj7**
                 But didn't want ____ to leave his name.

                     Em7   **Dm7**   **Em7**   **Am7**
                 I guess two can play the game of part time lovers.

                     Dm7 **Em7**   **Am7**
                 You and me,   part time lovers.

                            Dm7 **Em7**   **Am7**   **N.C.**
                 But, she and he,   part time lovers.

                        Am7   **G**
Outro   ‖: Da, da, da, da, da, da, da, da.

                 Fmaj7   **Em7**
                    Da, da, da, da, da, da, da, da.

                 Dm7   **Em7**
                    Do, do, do, dum, ____ dum, da, da, da, da,

                 Am7   **Dm7** **Em7**
                 Da, da, da.   :‖   *Repeat and fade*

Shoo Be Doo Be Doo Da Day

Words and Music by
Stevie Wonder, Sylvia Moy
and Henry Cosby

Melody:

Your pre-cious sweet - heart,   she's so   faith - ful, __

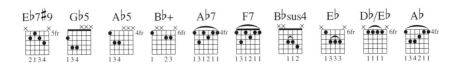

Intro
```
|N.C.(Eb7#9)    |        |        |
|Eb7#9          |        |        |
|Gb5  Ab5  Bb+  |
```

Verse 1

             Eb7#9   Ab7
Your precious sweet - heart, she's so faithful,

    Eb7#9
She's so true, oh, yeah.

                  Ab7
Her dreams are tumblin', her world is crumblin'

    Eb7#9
Because of you, uh huh.

            Ab7   F7
One day you'll hurt ___ her just once ___ too much,

Bbsus4   Eb   Gb5 Ab5   Bb+
And when you fin'ly lose your ten - der _____ touch,

Hey, hey.

Chorus 1

Db/Eb   Eb
Shoo-be-doo-be-doo-be-doo-da-day.

Db/Eb   Ab   Eb
Her feet may wander, her heart may stray, oh yeah.

Db/Eb   Eb
Shoo-be-doo-be-doo-be-doo-da-dee.

Db/Eb   Ab   Eb
You gonna send ___ your baby straight ___ to me.

Verse 2

       Eb7#9   Ab7
I'm gonna give her all the lovin'

       Eb7#9
Within my heart, oh, yeah.

             Ab7
I'm gonna patch up ev'ry sin - gle little dream

     Eb7#9
You tore apart. ___ Understand me?

       Ab7   F7   Bbsus4
And when she tells you she's cried her last tear,

       Eb   Gb5   Ab5   Bb+
Heaven knows ___ I'm gonna be some - where ___ near, ___ oh yeah.

Chorus 2

Db/Eb   Eb
Shoo-be-doo-be-doo-be-doo-da-day.

Db/Eb   Ab   Eb
Her feet may wander, her heart may stray, baby.

Db/Eb   Eb
Shoo-be-doo-be-doo-be-doo-da-dee.

Db/Eb   Ab   Eb
Love's gon' send your baby straight ___ to me.

Eb7#9
Yeah, mm, yeah, you'd better listen to me, yeah, yeah.

Verse 3

Eb7#9   Ab7
Heart aches are callin', tears ___ are fallin'

Eb7#9
Because of you, hey, yeah.

                                        Ab7
And when you're gone, you know I'm ___ the one

Eb7#9
To go to her rescue. Baby, you didn't know that thing.

                     Ab7   F7   Bbsus4
You're gonna leave ___ her once too many times,

                   Eb
And when you come ___ back

                  Gb5   Ab5 Bb+
That girl's gonna be mine, all mine.

Hey, hey.

Outro-Chorus

    Db/Eb   Eb
‖: Shoo-be-doo-be-doo-be-doo-da-day.

Db/Eb   Ab   Eb
Her feet may wander, her heart may stray, oh yeah.

Db/Eb   Eb
Shoo-be-doo-be-doo-be-doo-da-dee.

Db/Eb   Ab
Love's gonna send ___ your baby

     Eb
Straight ___ to me. :‖ *Repeat and fade w/ lead voc. ad lib.*

A Place in the Sun

Words and Music by
Ronald Miller and Bryan Wells

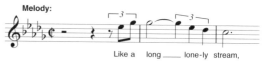

Melody:

Like a long ___ lone-ly stream,

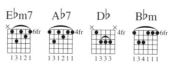

Ebm7 Ab7 Db Bbm

Intro
| Ebm7 | Ab7 | Db | |

Verse 1

   Ebm7   Ab7
Like a long, lonely stream,

  Db   Bbm
I keep runnin' towards a dream,

 Ab7   Db
Mov - in' on, mov - in' on.

  Ebm7   Ab7
Like a branch on a tree,

  Db   Bbm
I keep reachin' to be free,

 Ab7   Db
Mov - in' on, mov - in' on.

Chorus 1

     Ebm7   Ab7
There's a place ___ in the sun

    Db   Bbm
Where there's hope for ev'ryone,

   Ab7   Db
Where my poor restless heart's gotta run.

     Ebm7   Ab7
There's a place ___ in the sun

    Db   Bbm
And be - fore my life is done,

   Ab7   Db
Gotta find me a place in the sun.

Verse 2

                    E♭m7   A♭7
                    Like an old dusty road,

                    D♭   B♭m
                    I get weary from the load,

                    A♭7   D♭
                    Mov - in' on, mov - in' on.

                    E♭m7   A♭7
                    Like this tired troubled earth,

                    D♭   B♭m
                    I've been rollin' since my birth,

                    A♭7   D♭
                    Mov - in' on, mov - in' on.

Chorus 2   *Repeat Chorus 1*

                            D♭   E♭m7   A♭7
Interlude   *Spoken: You know, when times are bad and you're feeling sad,*

                            D♭
                    I want you to always remember.

Outro-Chorus   *Repeat Chorus 1 and fade*

Ribbon in the Sky

Words and Music by
Stevie Wonder

Oh ___ so long _____ for this night I prayed, _

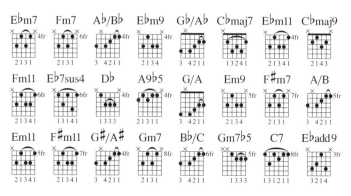

Intro

‖: E♭m7 │ Fm7 A♭/B♭ │ E♭m7   │ Fm7   A♭/B♭ :‖
│ E♭m7 │ Fm7 A♭/B♭ │ E♭m9 G♭/A♭ │ C♭maj7 G♭/A♭ │

Verse 1

E♭m7   Fm7   A♭/B♭
Oh, ___ so long for this night I prayed,

E♭m7   Fm7   A♭/B♭
That a star would guide you my way.

E♭m7   Fm7   A♭/B♭
To ___ share with me this special day,

E♭m11   G♭/A♭   C♭maj9 G♭/A♭
Where a ribbon's in the sky ___ for our love.

Verse 2

E♭m7   Fm11   A♭/B♭
If ___ allowed, may I touch your hand?

E♭m11   Fm11   A♭/B♭
And if pleased, may I once a - gain?

E♭m11   Fm11 A♭/B♭
So ___ that you too will under - stand,

E♭m11   G♭/A♭   D♭
There's a ribbon in the sky ___ for our love.

Verse 3

Ebm7　Fm11　Ab/Bb
Do, _____ do.

Ebm11　　　　　　　　　　　　　　　　Fm11
Mm, do, do, do, do, do, do, do, do, do, do, do, do, do, do,

Ab/Bb
Do, do, do, do.

Ebm11　Fm11　Ab/Bb
Mm, ___ do, ___ do, ___ dum.

Ebm11　Gb/Ab　A9b5　G/A
Do, _____ mm.

Verse 4

Em9　F#m7　A/B
This is not a coinci - dence,

Em11　　　　　F#m11　A/B
And far more than a lucky　chance.

Em11　　　F#m7　　A/B
But what is that was always meant,

Em11　　　　　G/A　　　　　G#/A#
Is our ribbon in the sky ___ for our love, love.

Verse 5

　　　　　　Fm11　　　　Gm7　　　Bb/C
We can't lose ___ with God ___ on our side.

Fm11　　　　　　　Gm7　　Bb/C
We'll find strength in each tear we cry.

　　　　Fm11　　Gm7　　　　Bb/C
From now on it will be ___ you and I,

　　　Fm11　　　　　Ab/Bb　　　Gm7b5　　　C7
And our ribbon in the sky, ___ ribbon ___ in the sky,

　　Fm7　　　　　　Ab/Bb　　　Fm11
A rib - bon in the sky　for our love.

Verse 6

　　　Gm7　　Bb/C
Ah, ooh, ___ do.

Fm11
Mm, do, do, do, do, do, do, do, do, do, do, do, do, do, do,

Gm7　　　　Bb/C
Do, do, do, do, ___ mm.

　　Fm11　Gm7
Mm, _____ mm.

　　　　Fm11　　　　Ab/Bb　　　Ebadd9
There's a rib - bon in the sky　for our love.

Send One Your Love

Words and Music by
Stevie Wonder

Melody:

Oh, _____

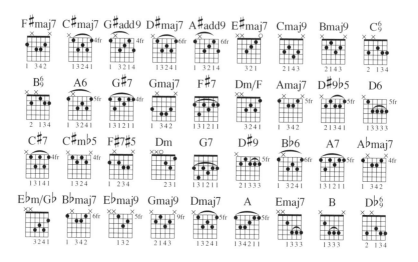

Intro

F#maj7 C#maj7 G#add9		D#maj7 A#add9
E#maj7 Cmaj9	Bmaj9	
F#maj7 C#maj7 G#add9		D#maj7 A#add9
Oh,   oh,

| Emaj7 C6/9 | B6/9 | |
Oh,   oh.

Chorus 1

A6
Send her your love

G#7   Gmaj7
With a dozen roses.

F#7   Dm/F
Make sure that she knows it,

Gmaj7   Amaj7
With a flower from your ___ heart.

A6
Show him your love,

G#7   Gmaj7
Don't hold back your feelings.

F#7   Dm/F
You don't need a reason

Gmaj7   Amaj7 D#9♭5
When it's straight from the heart.

Verse 1

D6   C#7
I've heard so many people say

C#m7♭5   F#7#5
That the days of ro - mance are no more,

Dm   G7
And people ___ falling in love

A6   D#9
Is so old fash - ioned.

D6
But waiting are they,

C#7   C#m7♭5
The day ___ they once let slip away,

F#7#5   Dm
Hiding need to fulfill

G7   C§   B§
Their de - sire for love's pas - sion.

Chorus 2

                    A6
Send her your love

G#7   **Gmaj7**
With a dozen roses.

F#7   **Dm/F**
Make sure that she knows it,

Gmaj7   **Amaj7**
With a flower from your ___ heart.

              A6
Show him your love,

G#7   **Gmaj7**
Don't hold back your feelings.

F#7   **Dm/F**
You don't need a reason

Gmaj7   **Amaj7 D#9b5**
When it's straight from the heart.

Verse 2

D6   **C#7**
I know that people say

          C#m7b5 **F#7#5**
Two hearts beating as one is un - real,

       Dm   **G7**   **A6**   **D#9**
And can on - ly happen in make-believe sto - ries.

     D6   **C#7**
But so blind they all must be

          C#m7b5   **F#7#5**
That they cannot believe ___ what they see,

       Dm   **G7**   **C6/9** **B6/9**
For around ___ us are mir - acles of love's glo - ry. Hey!

Harmonica Solo

B♭6	A7	A♭maj7	G7	
(Mm,	mm,	mm,	mm,	

E♭m/G♭	A♭maj7	B♭maj7	
Mm,	mm,	mm. Hey, yeah, yeah, yeah.)	

Chorus 3

                        B♭6
Show him your ___ love,

A7   A♭maj7
Don't hold back your feelings.

G7   E♭m/G♭
You don't need a reason

A♭maj7   B♭maj7
When it's comin' from your heart,

Amaj7 A♭maj7 E♭maj9 B♭maj7
Ah,   ah,   ah, ah,

Amaj7 A♭maj7 E♭maj9 B♭maj7
Ah,   ah,   ah, ah, ooh,

Amaj7 A♭maj7 E♭maj9
Ah,   ah,   ah, ah.

Gmaj9 Dmaj7 A
Ah.   Oh,   oh,

   Emaj7 B   F♯maj7 D♭§ C§
Oh, ___ oh, oh, ___ oh. ___ Hey!

Outro

‖: B♭6	A7	A♭maj7	G7	
E♭m/G♭	A♭maj7	B♭maj7	:‖	*Play 4 times*
B♭6			‖	

Signed, Sealed, Delivered I'm Yours

Words and Music by Stevie Wonder,
Syreeta Wright, Lee Garrett
and Lula Mae Hardaway

Melody:

Like a fool I went and stayed _ too long. _

(Capo 1st fret)

E   E7   E6   E5   Esus4   E*   C#m7   A   A/B   E7*

Intro

| E E7 E6 E5 | Esus4 E* | | E E7 E6 E5 | Esus4 E* |

Hey, hey.   Oh yeah, ba - by.

Verse 1

E*   C#m7
Like a fool I went and stayed ____ too long.

E*   C#m7
Now I'm wond'rin' if your love's still ____ strong.

      A
Ooh, ba - by, here I am,

A/B   E E7 E6 E5 Esus4 E*
Signed, sealed, delivered, I'm yours.   Mm.

Verse 2

E*   C#m7
Then that time I went and said ____ goodbye,

E*   C#m7
Now I'm back and not ashamed to cry.

      A
Ooh, ba - by, here I am,

A/B   E*
Signed, sealed, delivered, I'm yours. ____ Ah.

Chorus 1

        E*   **E7***
Here I am ___ baby,   woh.

A   **A/B**   **E* E7***
You got my future in your hands.   Ah.

A   **A/B**   **E   E7**
(Signed, sealed, de - livered, I'm yours.)

A   **A/B E***   **E7***
Here I am, baby,   ah,

A   **A/B**   **E* E7***
You got my future in your hands.   Hey.

A   **A/B**   **E   E7**
(Signed, sealed, de - livered, I'm yours.)

A   **A/B**
   I've done a lot of foolish things

E E7   **E6**   **E5**   **Esus4 E***
   That I really did - n't mean.   Ah, hey.

E   **E7 E6**   **E5 Esus4 E***
   Yeah, yeah,   didn't I?   Oh, ___ baby.

Verse 3

E*   **C♯m7**
   Seen a lot of things in this ___ old world, (Ooh.)

E*   **C♯m7**
   When I touch the baby, baby girl.

      A
Ooh, ba - by, here I am,

A/B   **E E7 E6 E5**   **Esus4 E***
Signed, sealed, delivered, I'm yours.   I'm yours.

Verse 4

E*   **C♯m7**
   Oohee, baby, set my soul ___ on fire, (Ooh.)

      E*   **C♯m7**
That's ___why I know you're my only, on - ly desire.

      A
Ooh, ba - by, here I am,

A/B   **E***
Signed, sealed, delivered, I'm yours.

Chorus 2

        E*   E7*
Here I am ___ baby,   woh,

A   A/B   E   E7*
You got my future in your hands. ___ baby.

A   A/B   E   E7
(Signed, sealed, de - livered, I'm yours.)

A   A/B E*   E7*
Here I am, baby,   ah,

A   A/B   E*   E7*
You got my future in your hands. ___ baby.   Yeah.

A   A/B   E   E7
(Signed, sealed, de - livered, I'm yours.)

A   A/B
I've done a lot of foolish things

E E7   E6   E5   Esus4 E*
That I really did - n't mean.

            E E7   E6 E5 Esus4 E*
I can feel for ya baby. But yeah, ah.   With the future.

          E7*
Got the future baby.   Ah.

       E7
(Here I am baby,.)

A   A/B E*   E7*
Here I am ___ baby.

A   A/B   E   E7
(Signed, sealed, de - livered, I'm yours.)

        A   A/B   E* E7*
Hey, ___ here I am ba - by.   Get it.

A   A/B   E*   E7*
(Signed, sealed, de - livered, I'm yours.) ___ (Yeah.)

        A   A/B E* E7*
Ooh, ___ ooh, baby here I am baby.

A   A/B   E*   E7*
(Signed, sealed, de - livered, I'm yours.) ___ (Yeah.) *Fade out*

Skeletons

Words and Music by
Stevie Wonder

Melody:

Skel-e-tons in ___ your clos - et ___

E♭m7

13121

Intro   ‖: E♭m7 | | | :‖

Verse 1
E♭m7
Skeletons in your closet itchin' to come outside,

Messin' with your conscience in a way your face can't hide.

Oh, things are gettin' real funky down at the old corral.

And it's not the skunks that are stinkin', it's the stinkin' lies you tell.

Chorus 1

E♭m7
   What did your mama tell you 'bout lies?

She said it wasn't polite to tell a white one.

What did your daddy tell you 'bout lies?

He said one white one turns into a black one.

Verse 2

E♭m7
So,   it's gettin' ready to blow. It's gettin' ready to show.

Somebody shot off at the mouth, and we're gettin' ready to know.

It's gettin' ready to drop. It's gettin' ready to shock.

Somebody done turned up the heater, and it's gettin' ready to pop.

Interlude

‖: N.C. | | | | :‖
| Em♭7 | | | |

Verse 3

E♭m7
Crevices in your pantry, now what do we have in here?

Havin' a daytime nightmare has always been your biggest fear.

Things are gettin' real crucial up the old wazoo.

Yet you cry, "Why am I the victim?" When the culprit's, Y.O.U.

Chorus 2   *Repeat Chorus 1*

Verse 4   E♭m7
                So,   it's gettin' ready to blow. It's gettin' ready to show.

Somebody shot off at the mouth, and we're gettin' ready to know.

It's gettin' ready to drop. It's gettin' ready to shock.

Somebody done turned up the heater, and it's gettin' ready to pop.

It's gettin' ready to seep. You're gettin' ready to freak.

Somebody picked up the talk box and gettin' ready to speak.

It's gettin' ready to jive. It's gettin' ready to gel.

Somebody done gone let the lid off, and it's gettin' ready to smell.

They're gettin' ready to deal. You're gettin' ready to ill.

Somebody just dropped the big dime. They're gettin' ready to squeal.

It's gettin' ready to turn. We're gettin' ready to learn.

Somebody fired up the brimstone. You're gettin' ready to burn.

It's gettin' ready to shake. You're gettin' ready to ache.

Somebody snitched to the news crew. It's gettin' ready to break.

You're gettin' ready to lie. They're gettin' ready to spy.

Somebody's been put on the hot seat. They're gettin' ready to fry.

Outro   ‖: E♭m7 | | | :‖ *Repeat and fade*

Sir Duke

Words and Music by
Stevie Wonder

Melody:

Mu - sic is a world with - in it - self

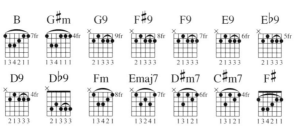

Intro ‖: N.C. | | | :‖

Verse 1
    B   **G#m**
Music is a world with - in itself
    G9   **F#9**
With a language we all understand,
    B   **G#m**
With an equal opportu - nity
    G9   **F#9 F9**
For all to sing, dance and clap their hands.

Pre-Chorus 1
          E9   **Eb9**   **D9**   **Db9**
But just be - cause a record has a groove,
    D9   **Eb9** **E9**
Don't make it in the groove.
        Eb9   **D9**   **Db9**
But you can tell right a - way at let - ter A
    D9 **Eb9 E9** **F9 F#9**
When the peo - ple start to move.

Chorus 1
    B   **Fm**
They can feel it all over.
Emaj7   **D#m7 C#m7 F#**
They can feel it all   over   people.
    B   **Fm**
They can feel it all over.
Emaj7   **D#m7 C#m7 F#**
They can feel it all   over, people go!

Interlude 1	‖: N.C. | | | :‖		

Verse 2

  B   **G♯m**
Music knows it is and always will be

    G9   **F♯9**
One of the things that life just won't quit.

  B   **G♯m**
But here are some of music's pioneers

         G9   **F♯9**   **F9**
That time will not allow us to forget, ___ now.

Pre-Chorus 2

            E9   **E♭9** **D9**   **D♭9**
For there's Basie, Miller, Satchmo,

        D9   **E♭9** **E9**
And the king of all, Sir   Duke.

              E♭9   **D9**   **D♭9**
And with a voice like Ella's ring - ing out,

        D9 **E♭9** **E9** **F9**   **F♯9**
There's no way the   band could lose.

Chorus 2

    B   **Fm**
‖: You can feel it all over.

  Emaj7   **D♯m7** **C♯m7** **F♯**
  You can feel it all   over   people. :‖ *Play 3 times*

  B   **Fm**
  You can feel it all over.

  Emaj7   **D♯m7** **C♯m7** **F♯**
  You can feel it all   over me, yeah, go, go!

Interlude 2   *Repeat Interlude 1*

Chorus 3

    B   **Fm**
‖: You can feel it all over.

  Emaj7   **D♯m7** **C♯m7** **F♯**
  You can feel it all   over   people. :‖ *Play 5 times*

  B   **Fm**
  You can feel it all over.

  Emaj7   **D♯m7** **C♯m7** **F♯**
  Ev'rybody all   over,   people go!

Outro   *Repeat Interlude 1*

Superstition

Words and Music by
Stevie Wonder

Tune down 1/2 step:
(low to high) E♭ - A♭ - D♭ - G♭ - B♭ - E♭

Melody:

Ver - y su - per - sti - tious, _

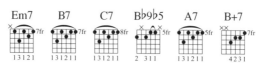

Em7   B7   C7   B♭9♭5   A7   B+7

Intro

N.C. | | | | |
| Em7 | | | | |

Verse 1

> Em7
> Very supersti - tious, writing's on the wall.
>
> Very superstitious, ladder's 'bout to fall.
>
> Thirteen month old baby broke the looking glass.
>
> Seven years of bad luck, the good things in your past.

Chorus 1

>   B7   C7
> When you believe ___ in things
>
>   B7   B♭9♭5   A7
> That you don't ___ understand ___ then you suf - fer.
>
> B+7   Em7
> Superstition ain't the way. ___ Hey, hey.

Verse 2

>   Em7
> Ooh, very supersti - tious, wash your face and hands.
>
> Rid me of the problem, do all that you can.
>
> Keep me in a daydream, keep me goin' strong.
>
> You don't wanna save me, sad is my song.

		B7			C7	

Chorus 2   When you believe ____ in things

          B7   **B♭9♭5**   **A7**

You don't ____ understand ____ then you suf - fer.

B+7   **Em7**

   Superstition ain't the way. ____ Hey, hey.

Interlude | **B7**   **C7** | **B7**   **B♭9♭5** | **A7** | **B+7** |

                | **Em7** | | | |

                           Em7

Verse 3   Very supersti - tious, nothing more to say.

Very superstitious, the devil's on his way.

Thirteen month old baby, mm, broke the looking glass.

Seven years of bad luck, good things in your past. Mm.

                   B7   **C7**

Chorus 3   When you believe ____ in things

               B7   **B♭9♭5**   **A7**

That you don't ____ understand ____ and you suf - fer.

B+7   **Em7**

   Superstition ain't the way. ____ No, no, no.

Outro   ‖: **Em7** | | | :‖ ***Repeat and fade***

Superwoman
(Where Were You When I Needed You)

Words and Music by
Stevie Wonder

Melody:

Mar - y wants to be a sup - er - wom - an, _____

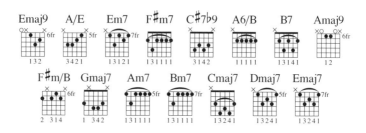

Verse 1

Emaj9   A/E   Emaj9
Mary wants to be super - wom - an,

Em7   A/E   Em7
But is that really in her head?

F♯m7
But I ____ just want to live each day

C♯7♭9   F♯m7
To love her for what she is.

A6/B   B7
Mm, ____ hmm. Mm.

Verse 2

Emaj9   A/E   Emaj9
Mary wants to be another movie star,

Em7   A/E   Em7
But is that really in her mind?

F♯m7
And all the things she wants to be,

C♯7♭9   F♯m7   A6/B
She needs to leave behind.

Chorus 1

Emaj9
But, very well,

Amaj9   F#m/B   Emaj9
I be - lieve I know you very well.

Amaj9   F#m/B   Gmaj7
Wish that you knew me too very well,

Am7   Bm7   Cmaj7
And I think I can deal with ev'ry - thing

Dmaj7   Emaj7
Going through your head.

Emaj9   Amaj9   F#m/B Emaj9
Very well, ___ and I think I can be very well.

Amaj9   F#m/B   Gmaj7
Wish that you knew me too very well,

Am7   Bm7   Cmaj7
And I think I can cope with ev'ry - thing

Dmaj7   Emaj7
Going through your head.

Verse 3

Emaj9   A/E   Emaj9
Mary wants to be a super - wom - an,

Em7   A/E Em7
And try to boss the bull around.

F#m7
But does ___ she really think

C#7b9   F#m7   A6/B
She'll get ___ by with a dream?

Verse 4

Emaj9   A/E   Emaj9
My woman wants to be a super - wom - an,

Em7   A/E Em7
And I just had to say good - bye

F#m7   C#7b9   F#m7   A6/B
Be - cause I can't spend all my hours start to cry.

Chorus 2   *Repeat Chorus 1*

Chorus 3

        Emaj9   **Amaj9**   **F#m/B**   **Emaj9**
Very well, ___ da, doo, da, da, doo, dum, very well.

      Amaj9 **F#m/B**   **Gmaj7**
Wish you knew me too very well,

     Am7   **Bm7**   **Cmaj7**
And I wish I could think of ev'ry - thing

     Dmaj7   **Emaj7**
Going through your head.

     Emaj9   **Amaj9**
Very well, da, dum, dum,

     F#m/B   **Emaj9**
Da, dum, dum, da, dum, dum.

     Amaj9   **F#m/B**   **Gmaj7**
Da, dum, dum, da, dum, dum, very well.

     Am7   **Bm7**   **Cmaj7**
And I think I can deal with ev'ry - thing

     Dmaj7   **Emaj7**
Going through your head.

That Girl

Words and Music by
Stevie Wonder

Intro

| (Drum) | | N.C. | | B♭m7 | E♭7#5#9 | |
||: A♭m9 | D♭13/A♭ | Emaj7/A♭ | D♭m7 Emaj7 E♭m7 :|| |

Verse 1

A♭m9   D♭13/A♭
That girl thinks that she's so fine

Emaj7/A♭   D♭m7 Emaj7 E♭m7
That soon she'll have my mind.

A♭m9   D♭13/A♭
That girl thinks that she so smart

Emaj7/A♭   D♭m7 Emaj7 E♭m7 D♭m7
That soon she'll have my heart.

G♭   D♭m7
She thinks, in no time flat,

    B♭m7   E♭7#5   A♭m9
That she'll be free and clear ___ for start

A13sus4   Dmaj9
With her emotional res - cue of love

      Gmaj9   C/G♭ D/G♭ E/G♭
That you leave ___ torn apart.

Verse 2

A♭m9   D♭13/A♭
That girl thinks that she's so bad,

    Emaj7/A♭   D♭m7 Emaj7 E♭m7
She'll change my tears to joy from sad.

A♭m9   D♭13/A♭
She says she keeps the upperhand,

Emaj7/A♭   D♭m7 Emaj7 E♭m7 D♭m7
'Cause she can please her man.

G♭   D♭m7
She doesn't use her love to make him weak,

     B♭m11   E♭7#5#9   A♭m9
She uses love to keep ___ him strong,

A13sus4   Dmaj9
And inside me there's no ___ room for doubt

     Gmaj9   C/G♭ D/G♭   E/G♭
That it won't ___ be long ___ before I tell her that I...

Chorus 1

D♭13sus4   B♭m7/A♭
Love her, that I want her,

     D♭9sus4   A♭13sus4
That my mind, soul and body needs her.

    A♭7#5♭9   D♭13sus4   B♭m7/A♭
Tell her that I'd love to, that I want to,

     D♭9sus4   A♭13sus4   A♭7#5♭9 D♭m9 B♭m7♭5 E♭7#9
That I need to do all that I have to be in her love.

Bridge

D♭m7♭5   Gmaj7/B
I've been hurting for a long time.

D♭m7♭5   Gmaj7/B   A♭m11
You've been playing for a long time, you know it's true.

D♭m7♭5   Gmaj7/B
I've been holding for a long time,

D♭m7♭5   Gmaj7/B
And you've been running for a long time.

    A♭m9   B♭m7♭5   A13
It's bound to do, what we've got to do.

Harmonica Solo *Repeat Verse 1 (Instrumental)*

Verse 3

Abm9   Db13/Ab
That girl knows ev'ry single man

Emaj7/Ab   Dbm7 Emaj7 Ebm7
Would ask her for her hand,

Abm9   Db13/Ab
But she says her love is much too deep

Emaj7/Ab   Dbm7 Emaj7 Ebm7 Dbm7
For them to understand.

Gb   Dbm7
She says her love has been crying out,

Bbm11 Eb7#5#9 Abm11
But her lover has - n't heard,

A13sus4   Dmaj9
But what she doesn't realize

      Gmaj9 C/Gb
Is that I've listened to ___ ev'ry word.

    D/Gb   E/Gb
That's why I know I'll tell her that I

Outro-Chorus

   Db13sus4 Bbm7/Ab
‖: Love her, that I want her,

   Db9sus4   Ab13sus4
That my mind, soul and body needs her.

Ab7#5b9 Db13sus4 Bbm7/Ab
Tell her that I love to, that I want to,

   Db9sus4   Ab13sus4
That I need to do all that I have ___ to,

   Ab7#5b9
To be in ___ her love. Tell her I... :‖ *Repeat and fade*
               w/ lead vocal ad lib.

Uptight
(Everything's Alright)

Words and Music by Stevie Wonder,
Sylvia Moy and Henry Cosby

Melody:

Ba - by,   ev - 'ry-thing is all   right. _

(Capo 4th fret)

A   G/A

123

Intro

| N.C.(drums) | | N.C.(A7) | | |
|:|: A | G/A | A | G/A | :|

Chorus 1

A   G/A
Baby, ev - 'rything is all right.

A   G/A
Uptight, out ___ of sight.

A   G/A
Baby, ev - 'rything is all right.

A   G/A
Uptight, out ___ of sight.

Verse 1

        A   G/A
I'm a poor ___ man's son from across the   railroad tracks.

       A   G/A
On - ly shirt I own is hangin' on my back.

          A   G/A
But I'm ___ the envy of ev'ry single guy,

        A   G/A
Since I'm ___ the apple of my ___ girl's eye.

        A   G/A
When we go out steppin' on the town ___ for awhile,

        A   G/A
My mon - ey's slow and my suits ___ are out of style.

        A   G/A
But it's all right if my clothes aren't new,

       A   G/A
Out ___ of sight, because my heart is true.

Chorus 2

        A   G/A
She says, "Baby, ev - 'rything is all right.

A   G/A
Uptight, out ___ of sight.

   A   G/A
Ba - by, ev - 'rything is all right.

A   G/A
Uptight and clean ___ out of sight.

Interlude   ‖: A |G/A   :‖ *Play 4 times*

Verse 2

      A   G/A
She's a pearl of a girl, I guess that's what you might say.

  A   G/A
I guess her folks brought her up ___ that way.

   A   G/A
The right side of the tracks, she was born ___ and raised,

      A   G/A
In a great ___ big old house full of butlers and maids.

    A G/A
She says, "No one is better than I."

  A   G/A
I ___ know I'm just an average guy.

   A   G/A
No football hero or smooth ___ Don Juan.

      A   G/A
Got emp - ty pockets, you see I'm a poor ___ man's son.

    A   G/A
Can't give her the things that mon - ey can buy,

    A   G/A
But I nev - er, never, never make my baby cry.

    A   G/A
And it's all right what I can't do,

    A   G/A
Out ___ of sight, because my heart is true.

Outro

      A G/A
She says, "Baby, ev - 'rything is all right.

  A   G/A
Uptight, clean ___ out of sight."

   A   G/A
‖: Ba - by, ev - 'rything is all right.

  A   G/A
Uptight clean ___ out of sight. :‖ *Repeat and fade*
                   w/ vocal ad lib.

You Haven't Done Nothin'

Words and Music by
Stevie Wonder

Melody:

We are a - mazed, _ but not a - mused _

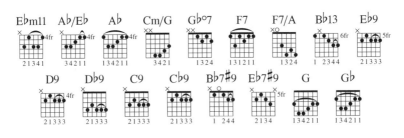

Intro

‖: N.C.(Ebm11) | :‖

‖: Ebm11 Ab/Eb |Ebm11 Ab/Eb :‖ *Play 4 times*

Verse 1

    Ebm11   Ab/Eb
We are amazed, but not amused

    Ebm11   Ab/Eb Ebm11 Ab/Eb
By all ___ the things you say that you ___ do,

Ebm11 Ab/Eb Ebm11   Ab/Eb
   Though much concerned, but not involved

     Ebm11   Ab/Eb Ebm11 Ab/Eb
With de - cisions that are made by ___ you.

Ebm11 Ab/Eb Ab
  But we are sick and tired

    Cm/G Gb°7 F7
Of hear - ing   your song,

     F7/A   Bb13
Telling how you were gonna change right from wrong,

     Eb9 D9   Db9 C9 Cb9 Bb7#9
'Cause if you really want to hear our ___ views,

      Eb7#9 Ab/Eb Eb7#9 Ab/Eb Eb7#9 Ab/Eb
You haven't done noth - in'.

Verse 2

E♭7♯9 A♭/E♭   E♭m11   A♭/E♭
            It's not too cool to be ridiculed,

   E♭m11   A♭/E♭ E♭m11 A♭/E♭ E♭m11 A♭/E♭
But you ___ brought this upon your - self.

    E♭m11   A♭/E♭
Though others tried to pacify,

    E♭m11   A♭/E♭   E♭m11   A♭/E♭
We want ___ the truth and nothing ___ else, ___ yea.

E♭m11 A♭/E♭ A♭   G   G♭   F7
    And we are sick and tired of hear - ing your song,

       F7/A   Bb13
Telling how you were gonna change right from wrong,

       E♭9 D9   D♭9 C9   B♭7♯9
'Cause if you really want to hear our views,

        E♭7♯9 A♭/E♭
You haven't done noth - in'.

E♭7♯9   A♭/E♭
Jackson Five, jaw along with ___ me,

  E♭7♯9   A♭/E♭ E♭7♯9   A♭/E♭
Say doo, doo, wop, yeah, ___ doo, doo, wop, oh,

E♭7♯9   A♭/E♭
Doo, doo, wop, mmm, hmm, mmm,

E♭7♯9   A♭/E♭
Doo, doo, wop, oh, ho, ho,

E♭7♯9   A♭/E♭   E♭7♯9
Doo, doo, wop, mmm, goin' doo,   doo, wop.

Verse 3

Ebm11   Ab/Eb   Ebm11
We would ____ not care to wake up to ____ the night - mare

            Ab/Eb   Ebm11 Ab/Eb Ebm11 Ab/Eb
That's becomin' real ____ life,

Ebm11   Ab/Eb   Ebm11
But when misled, who knows, a per - son's mind

            Ab/Eb Ebm11   Ab/Eb
Can turn as cold as ____ ice, ____ mmm, ____ hmm.

Ebm11   Ab   G Gb F7
Why do you keep on makin' us hear ____ your song,

        F7/A   Bb13
Tellin' us how you were changin' right from wrong?

          Eb9 D9   Db9 C9 Cb9   Bb7#9
'Cause if you really want to hear our ____ views,

      Ab Gb Eb7#9 Ab/Eb
You have - n't done nothin'.

    Eb7#9   Ab/Eb   Eb7#9   Ab/Eb
Yeah, ____ now, no, no noth - in', nothin'.

Eb7#9   Ab/Eb
Jackson Five, sing one mo' 'gin, ____ say,

Outro

    Eb7#9   Ab/Eb
‖: Doo, doo, wop, mmm, aha,

Eb7#9   Ab/Eb Eb7#9   Ab/Eb
Doo, doo, wop, oh, ____ doo, doo, wop, ho, ho, ho,

Eb7#9   Ab/Eb
Doo, doo, wop, sing it, Jack - ie. :‖ *Repeat and fade*
w/ lead vocal ad lib.

Yester-Me, Yester-You, Yesterday

Words by Ron Miller
Music by Bryan Wells

Melody:

What hap-pened to _____

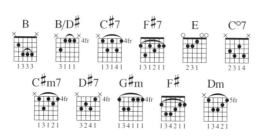

Intro

B	B/D♯	C♯7	F♯7	B	E

Yes - ter - me, yester-you, yester - day.

Verse 1

B	C°7	C♯m7	F♯7	B

What happened to the world we knew,

C♯m7　　　　F♯7

When we would dream and scheme

B　　　D♯7　G♯m

And wile the time a - way,

C♯7　　F♯7　　　B　E

Yester-me, yester-you, yester - day?

Verse 2

B	C°7	C♯m7	F♯7	B

Where did it go, that yester - glow,

C°7　C♯m7　　　F♯7

When we could feel the wheel

B　　　D♯7　G♯m

Of life ___ turn ___ our way,

C♯7　　F♯7　　　B　E

Yester-me, yester-you, yester - day?

GUITAR CHORD SONGBOOK

Verse 3

B   C°7   C#m7   F#7
I had a dream, ___ so did you.

B   D#7 G#m
Life was warm ___ and love ___ was true.

C#7   F#7 N.C.
Two kids who followed all the rules,

F#   E B/D#
Yes - ter-fools.

Dm C#m7   F#7   B
And now, now it seems those yester - dreams

C°7 C#m7   F#7   B
     Were just a cruel and foolish game

D#7 G#m   C#7   F#7   B   E
We used to play, yester-me, yester-you, yester - day.

Verse 4

B   C°7 C#m7   F#7
When I recall   what we had,

B D#7 G#m
I feel lost, ___ I feel sad,

C#7   F#7 N.C.
With nothing but the mem'ry of

F#   E B/D#
Yes - ter-love.

Dm C#m7   F#7   B
And now, now it seems those yester - dreams

C°7 C#m7   F#7   B
     Were just a cruel and foolish game

D#7 G#m   C#7   F#7   B
We had to play, yester-me, yester-you, yester - day.

E   B   C#7   F#7   B
Mmm, ___ yester-me, yester-you, yester-day.

E   B   C#7   F#7   B
Sing it with me, yester-me, yester-you, yester-day. *Fade out*

You Are the Sunshine of My Life

Words and Music by
Stevie Wonder

Melody:

You are the sun - shine of ___ my ___ life, ___

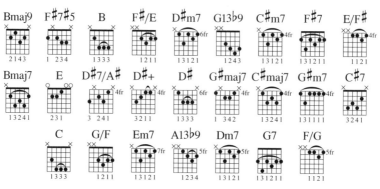

Intro ‖: Bmaj9 | |F#7#5 | :‖

Chorus 1

B   F#/E   D#m7 G13♭9
You are the sun - shine of my life,

C#m7   F#7   B C#m7 F#7
That's why I'll al - ways be around.

B   F#/E   D#m7 G13/9
You are the ap - ple of my eye.

C#m7   E/F#   B C#m7 F#7
Forever you'll ___ stay in my heart.

Verse 1

B   F#/E E/F# Bmaj7 F#/E E/F#
I feel like this ___ is the ___ be - ginning,

Bmaj7   E   E/F# D#7/A# D#m7 D#+ D#
'Though I've loved you for a mil - lion years.

G#maj7 C#maj7   D# G#m7
And if I thought our love ___ was ___ ending,

    C#7   F#7
I'd find ___ myself drowning in my own tears.

Whoa, whoa.

Chorus 2

B   F♯/E   D♯m7   G13♭9
You are the sun - shine of my life,

C♯m7   F♯7   B   C♯m7   F♯7
That's why I'll al - ways stay around.

B   F♯/E   D♯m7   G13♭9
You are the ap - ple of my eye.

C♯m7   E/F♯   B   C♯m7   F♯7
Forever you ___ stay in my heart.

Verse 2

B   F♯/E   E/F♯   Bmaj7   F♯/E   E/F♯
You must have known ___ that I ___ was ___ lonely,

Bmaj7   E   E/F♯   D♯7/A♯   D♯m7   D♯+   D♯
Because you came ___ to my ___ rescue.

G♯maj7   C♯maj7   D♯   G♯m7
And I know that his must ___ be ___ heaven.

          C♯7   F♯7
How could so ___ much love be inside of you?

G7
Whoa,

Chorus 3

   C   G/F   Em7   A13♭9
‖: You are the sun - shine of my life,

Dm7   G7   C   Dm7   G7
That's why I'll al - ways stay around.

C   G/F   Em7   A13♭9
You are the ap - ple of my eye.

Dm7   F/G   C   Dm7   G7
Forever you ___ stay in my heart.   :‖ *Repeat and fade*

You Will Know

Words and Music by
Stevie Wonder

Melody:

Lone - ly one of young, so bro-ken heart - ed. _

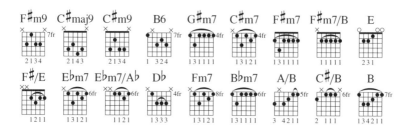

F#m9 C#maj9 C#m9 B6 G#m7 C#m7 F#m7 F#m7/B E
F#/E Ebm7 Ebm7/Ab Db Fm7 Bbm7 A/B C#/B B

Intro

‖: F#m9 |C#maj9 |F#m9 |C#m9 :‖

Verse 1

F#m9   C#maj9
Lonely one of young, so broken hearted,

F#m9   C#m9
Trav'ling down the rigid road of life,

F#m9   B6   G#m7
Using pharmaceutical ex - trac - tions

C#m7 F#m7   F#m7/B E
To find ____ the para - dise.

F#m9   C#maj9
Finds the high, but comes down feeling lower.

F#m9   C#m9
Gets down on their knees and starts to pray.

F#m9   B6 G#m7
Looking up to heaven for the an - swer,

    C#m7   F#m7   F#m7/B   E
They ___ hear ___ a voice ___ that says,

© 1987 JOBETE MUSIC CO., INC. and BLACK BULL MUSIC
c/o EMI APRIL MUSIC INC.
All Rights Reserved International Copyright Secured Used by Permission

GUITAR CHORD SONGBOOK

F#/E E   E♭m7
"You   will know,

E♭m7/A♭   D♭
Troubled heart, you'll know.

Fm7   B♭m7 Fm7 E♭m7
Problems have   so - lutions,

E♭m7/A♭   D♭
Trust and I will show.

    Fm7 B♭m7   E♭m7
Oh, ____ you will know,

E♭m7/A♭   D♭
Troubled heart, you'll know.

Fm7 B♭m7 Fm7 E♭m7
Ev'ry life   has   reason,

E♭m7/A♭   A/B C#/B B
For I made it so."

Verse 2

    F#m9   C#maj9
Single parent try'n' to raise their children,

F#m9   C#m9
But they would much rather not a - lone.

F#m9   B6   G#m7
Reaches out to find that special some - one

C#m7 F#m7   F#m7/B   E
To make ____ their house ____ a home.

F#m9   C#maj9
Finds someone, but no one is the right one.

F#m9   C#m9
Gets down on their knees and starts to pray.

F#m9   B6 G#m7
Looking up to heaven for the an - swer,

    C#m7   F#m7   F#m7/B   E
They ____ hear ____ a voice ____ that says,

Chorus 2

F♯/E E   E♭m7
"You   will know,

E♭m7/A♭   D♭
Lonely heart, you'll know.

Fm7   B♭m7 Fm7 E♭m7
Problems have   so - lutions,

E♭m7/A♭   D♭
Trust and I will show.

    Fm7 B♭m7   E♭m7
Hey, ___ you will know,

E♭m7/A♭   D♭
Lonely heart, you'll know.

Fm7 B♭m7 Fm7 E♭m7
Ev'ry life   has   reason,

E♭m7/A♭   A/B C♯/B B
For I made it so."

Outro-Chorus

                    E♭m7 E♭m7/A♭   **D♭**
‖: You'll know, ____ troubled heart you'll know.

Fm7   B♭m7 Fm7 E♭m7
Problems have   so - lutions,

E♭m7/A♭   D♭
Trust and I will show.

         Fm7 B♭m7   E♭m7
Hey, ___ you will know,

E♭m7/A♭   D♭
Troubled heart, you'll know.

Fm7 B♭m7 Fm7 E♭m7
Ev'ry life   has   reason,

E♭m7/A♭   D♭
For I made it so.

        Fm7 B♭m7   E♭m7
Oh, ___ you will know,

E♭m7/A♭   D♭
Lonely heart, you'll know.

Fm7   B♭m7 Fm7 E♭m7
Problems have   so - lutions,

E♭m7/A♭   D♭
Trust and I will show.

       Fm7 B♭m7   E♭m7
Hey, ___ you will know,

E♭m7/A♭   D♭
Lonely heart, you'll know.

Fm7 B♭m7 Fm7 E♭m7
Ev'ry life   has   reason,

E♭m7/A♭   A/B C♯/B B
For I made it so.   :‖ *Repeat and fade*

You Met Your Match

Words and Music by Stevie Wonder,
Lula Hardaway and Don Hunter

Hey, _____ you were good at play-in' the ___

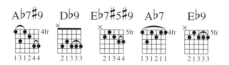

Intro

‖: N.C.(A♭7♯9) | :‖

Verse 1

A♭7♯9
Hey, you ___ were good at playin' the fox, girl.

When I was good, you threw me a bone.

But I ain't playin' hot for nobody.

Girl, just wait till I get you home,
D♭9
I'll show you the way to love somebody
E♭7♯5♯9
Like ___ you've never ever been shown.
A♭7
'Cause my love ___ lights burnin',
D♭9   A♭7
My whole life's yearnin' for you.

Verse 2   N.C.(E♭9)   A♭7♯9
Hey, baby, you play the part with Jimmy and Freddy.

You tried to make me look like a fool.

But I took care of Cindy and Susie

Just to show you I can be twice as cruel, baby.
D♭9
If you wanna learn how to love me
E♭7♯5♯9
I'll teach ___ you in my own private school.
A♭7
'Cause my love ___ lights burnin'
D♭9   A♭7
My whole life's yearning for you.

A♭7♯9
Chorus 1   (You met your match.) When you play with my affection.

(You met your match.) When you try to make me walk the line.

(You met your match.)When you decided you would hurt me.
N.C.
That's   when your grape fell from the vine, vine, vine, vine.

Verse 3
                  Ab7#9
Your mama told me that I better be mellow.

She said you're just a baby, maybe too green.

I told her Jimmy, Freddy, Teddy and Victor they knew better.

Mama, shake off that dream.
    Db9
Hey, I told her that you really were cookin'.
    Eb7#9
My love is burnin' for a turn at the steam.
        Ab7
Hey, 'cause my love ____ lights burnin',
  Db9   Ab7
My whole life's yearning for you.

               Ab7#9
Outro-Chorus ‖: (You met your match.) When you told me that you love me.

(You met your match.) When you told me that you won't let go.

(You met your match.) You met your match. You met your match.

You met your match. You met your match.

(You met your match, baby.) :‖ *Repeat and fade*
                                    w/ lead vocal ad lib.